DEUTSCHLAND: EIN WINTERMÄRCHEN

Published 2005
by

STACK
BOOKS

Smokestack Books
PO Box 408, Middlesbrough TS5 6WA
Tel : 01642 813997
e-mail : info@smokestack-books.co.uk
www.smokestack-books.co.uk

Cover painting by George Grosz
Author photo by Jo Mazelis

Cover design and print by
James Cianciaruso
james.cianciaruso@ntlworld.com

ISBN 0-9548691-1-7

Smokestack Books
gratefully acknowledges the support of
Middlesbrough Borough Council
and Arts Council North East.

Smokestack Books is a member of
Independent Northern Publishers
www.northernpublishers.co.uk

DEUTSCHLAND: EIN WINTERMÄRCHEN
by
Heinrich Heine

GERMANY: A WINTER'S TALE
Translated with introduction and notes
by
John Goodby

For exiles, refugees and asylum seekers everywhere

Acknowledgements

I would like to thank Lou Smith (Lydia Jäschke), who inspired and aided my first efforts at this translation. Credit for advancing the work beyond its modest beginnings go to Bébhinn NicLiam and Steve Kerry, whose advice and generous help, given over many years, saw me through the first draft. Despite its belated completion, I hope that what follows will persuade them to modify any charges of dilatoriness and to concur with the Italian proverb quoted by Redbeard in Caput 15: *chi va piano va sano*. I am also extremely grateful to Tom Cheesman of the Department of German at Swansea University, who improved the translation, weeded out howlers and blunders and comprehensively edited the apparatus of this book. Any errors which remain are, of course, entirely my own.

Thanks are also due to Professor Norma Rinsler, editor of *Modern Poetry in Translation* (New Series) issue no, 11, Summer 1997, for permission to use earlier versions of Caputs 6, 11 and 12 as well as the additional material on translating *Deutschland*. Without her encouragement at a critical time the full translation would not have seen the light of day.

Finally, I would like to record my gratitude to the Arts Council of Wales for the award of a Writers' Bursary in 1999, when the completed translation was fine-tuned, and much of the introduction and notes were written.

Introduction

The immediate inspiration for *Deutschland. Ein Wintermärchen*, Heine's witty mock-epic on the state of Germany, was a visit to Hamburg in October-December 1843. Heine had been in exile in Paris since May 1831, and it was the first time he had been back on German soil for twelve years; he was to return only once more, in 1844. The main purposes of the trip were to see his mother and sister, assuage his homesickness, and to meet Julius Campe, his publisher; but it also had the effect of showing him how much (and how little) life in Germany had changed during his absence. Liable to be arrested as a subversive in the German Confederation, however - particularly in the Prussian territories through which the route ran - Heine made the outward journey by the safer sea-route from Amsterdam to Hamburg, via Bremen. But he took the risk of returning by land, using false papers; and this journey, in reverse, supplied the itinerary for the poem's picaresque, episodic trail from the border near Aachen, via Cologne, Mühlheim, Unna, the Teutoberg Forest, Paderborn, Minden, Bückeburg, Hannover and Hagen to Hamburg.

On returning, Heine quickly completed the poem: he tells us that the poem was 'Geschrieben in Januar 1844'. It is in ballad metre, runs to just over two thousand lines, and is shaped into twenty-seven 'Caputs', or cantos - nineteen for the journey and eight for Hamburg. He published it later that year in *Neue Gedichte / New Poems*, where it concludes a section of poems titled *Zeitgedichte / Poems of our time* (or 'timely poems' - the term has a complexity which make it impossible to render satisfactorily in English) and it was also serialized, in accordance with Heine's hopes of reaching a larger audience than usual, in the Paris-German newspaper *Vorwärts!*, thanks to Heine's friendship with Karl Marx, its co-editor. The new collection signalled a significant return to poetic form for Heine who, though he saw himself primarily as a poet, had published no new collection since his *Buch der Lieder / Book of Songs* in 1827. Heine summed up *Deutschland* in this way in his letter of April 1844 to Campe:

> It captures the whole of the present German ferment in the boldest, most personal way. It is politics in the Romantic manner, and I hope it will sweep away, once and for all, the leaden bombast of today's would-be political poets. You know I'm not the kind to boast, but this time I'm sure I've produced a little work that will cause more furore than any popular pamphlet, and yet have the lasting value of a classic poem.

Heine's claims for *Deutschland* have, in many ways, been vindicated.
It is the supreme poem of the *Vormärz*, the period preceding the
1848-9 revolution, and is widely considered to be the most important
political poem in German. On the other hand, as a 'classic poem'
it sits rather awkwardly, like much that he wrote, with the earnest,
apolitical nature of the German literary tradition. We might also ask
what Heine meant by 'politics in the Romantic manner', and who
were the 'would-be political poets' ? More importantly, how did
Heine, previously known for the sweet-sour love lyrics of *Buch der
Lieder*, the antithesis of committed poetry, come to write a poem like
Deutschland ?

Harry Heine (the 'Heinrich' adopted on his grudging baptism as a
Lutheran in 1825) was born in 1797 to a middle-class Jewish family
in Düsseldorf, a liberal Rhineland city and one of the few in Germany
without a ghetto. He was brought up with his Catholic neighbours,
and was exposed to Christian, Jewish, German and French rationalist
and orthodox influences at a formative age. Napoleon's occupation of
the Rhineland in 1805 led to the abolition of civic disabilities on Jews.
But with the final defeat of France in 1815, there was a restoration
of the old European order, overseen by Prince Metternich of Austria.
This returned the three dozen German princes to their thrones,
reinstated the Bourbons in France, and instituted a Triple Alliance
of reactionary powers, Russia, Austria and Prussia, in order to keep
the spirit of revolution firmly crushed (the Alliance's moribund
nature is powerfully symbolised by the relics of the Magi in Cologne
Cathedral, described in Caput 6 of *Deutschland*). With the fall of
Napoleon, the Rhine provinces were handed to Prussia, which in 1823
reinstated penalties against the Jews living there.

Heine was already thirty-three when the first breach occurred in
this repressive edifice, with the July Revolution in France in 1830; a
bloodless overthrow of the Bourbons, followed by the installation of
a 'Citizen King', Louis Philippe. But Germany remained apathetic,
its middle-class and liberals too cowed and complacent to follow the
French example. Small wonder, then, that the radical Heine should
claim that the French were the 'chosen people' of the 'new religion
of our time', freedom, and that the Rhine was 'the Jordan which
separates the sacred land from the country of the Philistines'. Nor
was it surprising that he decided to go into voluntary exile in Paris the
following year, in May 1831 (he refers to this journey, towards warm
freedom rather than into the 'winter's tale' of Metternich's frozen
Germany, when he contrasts the Mülheim of 1844 with the same city
in 1831 in Caput 8). There was little to stay for: in 1827 he had been
imprisoned and then expelled from Würtemburg as an undesirable

while visiting his brother, and passed over for a professorship in Munich - the post going to the 'teutomaniac' Hans Ferdinand Massmann (who turns up, to be mocked, in Caput 11). As career prospects closed off, anti-Semitism, censorship and surveillance were closing in. Heine's wealthy uncle Salomon was no help, and his father had recently died. When news of the revolution came, Heine decided to try his luck as a freelance writer in Paris.

By 1830, Heine had a reputation as a poet in Germany, but a European one as a writer of prose and journalism. This was largely thanks to his *Reisebilder / Travel Sketches*, a series of innovative and subversively ironic works which, first published in 1825, ran to four volumes by 1831. When he arrived in Paris he was received with open arms - his acquaintance soon resembled a *Who's Who* of French artistic and political life - and he successfully set about creating a dual role for himself as interpreter of German culture and philosophy to the French, and of French politics to the Germans. *On the History of Philosophy and Religion in Germany* (1832) and *The Romantic School* (1835) duly appeared, along with scintillating journalism in the liberal German newspaper, the *Augsburger Zeitung*. As well as establishing Heine in France, these works also accomplished more serious aims: *The Romantic School*, for example, corrected Madame de Staël's *De l'Allemagne* (1810), until then the main French source of information about German culture, which had stereotyped Germany as a land of poets and philosophers and, Heine felt, reinforced reactionary Romantic clichés.

Yet during the 1830s Heine's poetry dried up. Moreover, liberating as France was, he remained deeply attached to Germany, even though its rulers rejected him with growing vehemence: on 10 December 1835 the German Federal Diet lumped Heine with the slightly younger 'Young Germany' group of writers as a dangerous author, whose past and future work was to be banned throughout the territories of the German Confederation. Perhaps understandably, the *amo* in Heine's *odi et amo* relationship with Germany often baffled the French: in Dumas' words, 'If Germany doesn't want [Heine] we'll adopt him. Unfortunately, Heine loves Germany more than she deserves.' What little poetry he did write in these years, apart from free verse experiments which proved a dead-end, remained within the narrow limitations of the *Buch der Lieder's* love lyrics. When a second edition of that book appeared in 1837, Heine admitted in the Preface that for several years he had found prose a more honest medium than verse. Nor did the prose always win admirers; *Ludwig Börne* (1839), a good example of Heine's gift for making enemies as well as friends, led to attacks on him for breaking ranks with the other radical German exiles. By now he had also acquired a partner, Mathilde, with costly tastes, and had begun to suffer from the paralysing illness which would kill him. Worst of all, his enthusiastic reception in Paris did not translate itself into economic security.

Nevertheless, during the late 1830s Heine had been trying to wrench his poetry out of the groove of predictability. A longish, unusually realistic poem of 1836, 'Der Tannhäuser, eine Legende' (the source for Wagner's opera) uses narrative and traveller's vignettes, in the manner of the *Reisebilder* prose. A richly imaginative prose tale, *Florentine Nights,* and an essay on Germanic folklore, also showed that he might be re-establishing contact with the sources of his inspiration. Yet what was new about the poems he began to write in the early 1840s was their realism. To some extent, realism was always implied in Heine's earlier lyrics, however confected, and despite the conventional imagery of butterflies, nightingales and flowers; pastoral presupposes sophisticated cosmopolites, and *Buch der Lieder's* poems are in the post-Romantic genre of Romantic irony. Alienation is built into their self-conscious, song-within-song structures, while a new urban world of getting and spending, of polite but icy society, lurks at their edges. But now the realism was foregrounded, and took a political cast.

One reason for this was that the new work had been catalysed by the 'leaden bombast of today's would-be political poets', as the letter to Campe puts it. This refers to the 'Young Germany' poets who had suddenly begun publishing agitprop verse - what became known as *Tendenzpoesie* (that is, poetry with a 'tendency', or political viewpoint). Heine was shocked by its crassness, which he felt was likely to do the causes they supported more harm than good (he may also have felt wrong-footed; with his reputation, shouldn't he have been there first ?). He cuttingly symbolized its inadequacies in a poem on one of them, Georg Herwegh, who is likened to an 'eisene Lerche' / 'iron lark'. Initially Heine's chief concern was to assert the rights of the aesthetic against the crudely propagandistic, the concrete image against the abstraction. The major fruit of this phase was *Atta Troll: Ein Sommmernachtstraum*, written in 1841 (with its title and twenty-seven caputs made up of quatrains, it is clearly the contrasting companion piece to *Deutschland*). Heine called *Atta Troll* 'the last free woodland song of Romanticism', which is fair enough, and the opening lines assert poetry's self-sufficient aesthetic autonomy. But precisely in doing this, they reveal the self-conscious rupture through which the political was gradually entering Heine's poetry; and, read carefully, *Atta Troll* turns out to be a thinly veiled, if richly musical allegory directed against the inflexibility of radicals like Börne.

Heine soon showed that he could be as direct as the *Tendenzgedichter*, while maintaining the quality of poems as poems. A famous piece on the brutally-suppressed Silesian weavers' strike of 1843, 'Die Schlesischen Webern' / 'The Silesian Weavers', for example, has a chant-like rhythm and a repeated refrain, but is a model of verbal economy and tellingly concrete imagery. Other *Zeitgedichte* were also written at this time, directed against targets such as the Prussian King, Friedrich Wilhelm IV, so that by the time of *Deutschland* the barrier between Heine's prose and poetry had, for the time being, been broken down, to the poetry's advantage. Heine would return to a purer lyric poetry in his last years, but for now the political imagination was no longer subordinate to lyric, and poured into it, allowing the poetry to be remade in the prose's dialogic, discursive image.

'Dialogic' is a useful term to bear in mind when reading *Deutschland*. Heine's self-divisions are, of course, notoriously complex and manifold - the socialist who was a parliamentary monarchist; the communist who feared the masses; the Jew who converted to Lutheranism; the anti-Romantic Romantic; the scourge of nationalism who was homesick and relied on Germanic material for his inspiration - the list could be extended almost indefinitely. But these were exploited far more than they were suffered, for creative purposes; that is, they have a textual, rather than a merely subjective-biographical importance. Their significance lies in the fact that Heine needed to inhabit such binaries in order to deconstruct them. Each term is treated as so entwined with the other that neither can stand on its own. So, *Deutschland* satirizes German backwardness and attacks Prussian ambition on the one hand; on the other, it hints at the libertarian principles on which a more just order might be built. But it also exposes contradictions lurking in this neat pairing; the narrator's homesickness and love for Germanic culture contrasts with his anger at repression, his love of high culture throws into relief the limitations of a purely utilitarian, economic form of freedom.

This constant interrogation is also a function of the poem's style. At a basic level, if its weather is dark and wintry, *Deutschland's* verbal texture is buoyed by the play of wit; here the medium, as Heine knew it had to be, is a good deal of the message. As Jeffrey Grossman argues, Heine's 'mix of styles, his shift of tones and registers, and his juxtaposing of discordant events and images work to evoke and satirize cultural norms and ideologies.' 'Mix' is crucial: Heine variously uses irony, polemic, mockery, calculated banality, joke, deflationary rhymes, character assassination, lyricism, nostalgia, magical realism, prophecy and scatalogical humour, creating a text which is *stylistically* dialogic, as well as through its many debates.

Similarly, the persona - for we should not speak of Heine 'himself' in the poem, even if the experience of the narrator is often coterminous with Heine's own - is inconsistent in his beliefs, and even downright evasive. Barker Fairley claims, dubiously, that Heine himself is the narrator of the poem, and that he 'speaks' as 'our fellow-man (sic)'. This is partly a question of intellectual fashions; however, as Peter Hohendahl puts it, 'We have at least to acknowledge the possibility that the unity of Heine as an author is a fiction.' Which is not to suggest that Heine is an irresponsible writer, interested only in surface, a precursor of one of the more superficial brands of postmodernism. If, at times, he seems impossibly contradictory, he is also consistent; there is a 'conflicted totality' to his work, in Hohendahl's useful phrase, which stems from its emancipatory impulse. Matthew Arnold, rightly referring to Heine's lifelong activity as 'a soldier in the war of the liberation of humanity', echoed the late poem 'Enfant perdu' in which Heine portrays himself as a sentry who has served for thirty years defending the ramparts of liberty and now falls, but 'fall[s] unbeaten'. Although the poem's self-dramatizing should not be taken wholly at face value, it is valuable in attributing the sentry's death to self-division - 'only my heart it was that broke'. That image sums up the price paid by the radical writer who is also an aesthete, who insists on understanding a range of identities, who regards selfhood as process and therefore as a kind of perpetual performance. Heine knew that a protean quality was necessary in order to fully appreciate the flux of his times, but was also aware of the hugely taxing demands it made on his self-invention, the errors it could lead to, and the dangers of these being seen as lack of solidarity by one's allies.

Heine's synthesis of different, even opposed political positions, is difficult to assess, even today. At Bonn University in early 1820 he had joined the illegal nationalist student society, or *Burtschenschaft*; but after moving to Göttingen in autumn he was expelled, possibly because of anti-Semitism (this may be why Caput 10 pays a tribute to the friendly, if stolid, Westphalian students, but not those of Göttingen). In Berlin from 1821 to 1823, however, Heine attended Hegel's lectures, and became a liberal with increasingly radical leanings. Hegel taught Heine to view history in terms of the inexorable progress of reason; Heine, in turn, would infuse the Hegelian dialectic with the energies of Romanticism to arrive at a position close to that of the Left Hegelians a decade later - the 'politics in a Romantic manner' of the letter to Campe.

For a short period, while he was in Berlin, Heine also joined a society which sought to reconcile Jewish culture and Judaism with German

Enlightenment values. For a short time he even rejected his German identity (as Siegbert Prawer has shown, even when he kept it out of his writing he was always keenly aware of his Jewishness). Yet Heine was convinced that a German revolution could occur which would advance on the French example because it would be able to harness Hegel's insights into historical process, and, as a result, spread reason and liberty on an international scale. In supporting the struggle for emancipation - and Heine argued in 1828 that it must apply not only to Jews, but all oppressed peoples and races - he was a lateral, not a systematic thinker. An objection to reducing cultures to abstract ideas was pronounced from the first, and was linked to Heine's rejection of the moral puritanism which most radical reformers saw as necessary for success. This was to be a constant; throughout his career Heine viewed what he called the 'Nazarene' (as opposed to a 'Hellene', or sensualist mentality) as an internalized version of the repressive morality promulgated by Church and State. While he was occasionally capable of using sensualism to justify dubious political stances, Heine's belief that a restoration of the rights of the flesh could not be divorced from social and intellectual rights in the struggle for human liberty showed deep insight into the nature of human desires, and the dangers of revolutionary self-righteousness.

Such beliefs were reflected in Heine's interest, after 1828, in the Saint-Simonian sect. The Saint-Simonians preached a kind of socialist-sensualist doctrine, an anti-authoritarian utopia in which socio-economic goals were replaced by sensuous-erotic ones. The disillusioning aftermath of 1830 confirmed the appeal of Saint-Simonian ideals, and Heine fused it with his progressive philosophy. When, after 1832, the Saint-Simonians collapsed in a series of trials and exposures, Heine did not abandon his synthesis but incorporated into it ideas from the radical left, including those of the successors to 'Gracchus' Babeuf (the leading figure of the left in the French Revolution), known as the 'Conspiracy of Equals'. Heine rejected their Jacobinical mind-set, but respected the fact that they alone took seriously what to him was the most important right of all, the right not to starve (in an essay, 'Differing Conceptions of History', written in the mid-1830s, he had declared: '"Le pain est le droit du peuple," said Saint-Just, and that is the greatest declaration made in the entire French Revolution.')

As this shows, there was a pattern of oscillation in Heine's political beliefs, according to which he considered and then qualified radical political positions, trying to create, as he did so, a fresh synthesis likely to produce the emancipatory outcome he desired. His fluidly individual stances meant that he would never agree for long with the doctrine of any group, and he was always liable to be misunderstood when he attacked inflexibility, represented for him above all by ascetic rigour. Similar reservations affected his dealings with Marx's and Ruge's Left Hegelian group in the early 1840s when he again insisted that genuine freedom must have a cultural-sensual as well as material-theoretical dimension. After the onset of his paralysis, which coincided with the revolutionary outbreaks in Paris in 1848, Heine rejected his belief in the Hegelian progress of history. Nevertheless, he maintained an impulse for the struggle for liberty which, if anything, was more marked by its sympathy with the poor than before. (In the introduction to the French edition of *Lutetzia*, in 1855, Heine imagined a grocer, in a future communist society, using the pages of his Book of Songs to make paper bags, and says he would have no objection to this if they were to be 'filled with coffee or snuff' for 'poor old grandmothers, who in our present world of injustice perhaps have to do without such comforts').

There is little doubt that the writing of *Deutschland* coincided with the period of Heine's maximum optimism about the possibilities for communism, in 1843-4: 'Communism is favoured by the circumstance that the enemy it fights lacks moral stability and purchase. The established society of our time defends itself only out of an instinct of self-preservation; it has no belief in its own justification, no self-respect.' Communism was at this stage a purely theoretical notion advocated by a tiny group; the 'ferment' he mentioned to Campe was occurring in French politics, and there were rumblings in Germany itself. The optimism was enhanced by the warm, brief friendship Heine enjoyed with Karl Marx in 1844. The degree of mutual influence is still a matter for debate, but critics have convincingly shown that Heine's presentation of Germany as a topsy-turvy land, where illusion is taken for reality and vice versa, is very similar to Marx's in the introduction to his *Critique of Hegel's Philosophy of Right*, also dated Paris 1844. Heine, like Marx, begins his work with a critique of religion, 'the old denial hymn, / the Pie-in-the-Sky-Bye-and-Bye', and he is said to have been the source of Marx's phrase 'opium of the people'. It is likely that, for his part, Marx helped allay Heine's fears, temporarily, about the effect of revolutionary levelling on art. Whether he appreciated Heine's Saint-Simonian insistence in Caput 1 on 'Roses and myrtles, Beauty and Desire' as well as bread, or his mockery of empty 'wolvish' revolutionary rhetoric in Caput 12, is not known.

Structurally, it is this political armature which holds together *Deutschland's* heterogeneous materials and digressive methods. The conflict which, drives the poem, between a frozen Germany and an exuberant, confidently ironic self, is established at once. Caput 1 charts the ideological co-ordinates of a repressive order, the hypocrisy of organised religion, and the shining example of July 1830. The 'little harp-maiden's' resignation is critiqued by the narrator's socialistic desire to build heaven on earth, and his self-comparison with Antaeus at the end shows renewal through contact with his 'mother', the potentially resurgent energies of 'that dozing lout, / the People'. By way of another contrast, these ecstatic final lines are followed, in Caput 2, by the different kind of unity proposed by the nationalist fellow-passenger. There are all kinds of exchanges and switchings going on here; thus, the aesthetic-spiritual compensation for alienation which the harp-maiden's song represents, reappears, inverted, in the form of the crass power of the Prussian customs officials. This is then countered by the narrator's declaration of his hidden mental treasure - Hegel leavened with Saint-Simonianism. And this, in its turn, encounters the passenger's prediction of the Bismarckian terms of unification in 1870-71, demonstrating how Idealist philosophy could underpin repression, projecting Prussian expansionism in the guise of its own totalising imperatives, with military might thinly veiled by economic co-operation.

The opening, then, through assertion and challenge, critique and self-critique, establishes the terms by which *Deutschland* will proceed. These terms, which the reader soon learns to use, are more important than the details of the journey itself. These are pretty cursory - the River Rhine, Cologne cathedral, a fortress at Minden, a palace and a square in Bückeburg, various inns, a river or a forest, the miserable weather and roads. However, to complain about this is to miss the point, since it is the very sketchiness which generates a sense of the traveller's haste and the nimbleness of his commentary. Some details, of course, become leitmotifs - the eagle on the post-house crest in Caput 3, repeated in Caputs 18 and 21, or Caput 4's Cologne Cathedral, whose incompleteness is ironically seized on as the imperfectly perfect symbol of the German nation, both romantic fragment and monument to the defeat of medieval bigotry (it might have amused Heine to learn that a century and a half later the narrow alleys in the shadow of the cathedral would be full of sex shops). Similarly, the muddy roads of Caputs 8, 15 and 19 are not just ironic- as 'the fatherland's filth' they acquire a near-visionary intensity, and prepare the reader for the excremental vision of Caput 26. As in Hegel's view of history, the facts of Germany are manifestations of the narrator's mental Ideal, reflected in his thought-processes.

The most obvious target in *Deutschland*, from the border guards in Caput 2 to Friedrich Wilhelm IV's spies and dramatic tastes in Caput

27, is Prussia. It sums up all the malign aspects of national identity which Heine saw warring with its more positive ones. Every other target of the poem - nationalism, philosophy, institutionalized religion (Judaism and Christianity), romanticism, liberals, the middle classes - are viewed according to their place within this larger struggle. Heine intervenes in the particular battles, while recognizing that none can really be discussed in isolation. Heine's Jewishness, for example, plays a relatively small part in *Deutschland*. Nevertheless, the reference to the Jews of Hamburg in Caput 21 occurs in the context of the threatening-helpful Prussian eagle. Hamburg is clearly a place where Jews and Germans co-exist, and the Jews have the liberty to split into orthodox and liberal camps. This is an implicit critique, by juxtaposition, of the reactionary Germanness and anti-Semitism associated with Prussia. In the narrator's final comment, declaring his love for orthodox and liberal Jews, but his preference for smoked sprats over either, there is a Saint-Simonian insistence on the senses which amounts to a critique of organized religion. The encounter with the twelfth century Emperor Barbarossa, in Caput 16 is more obvious; Heine slyly has this great nationalist icon, after a century asleep, ask first of all after Moses Mendelsson, an eighteenth century German-Jewish sage noted for his attempt to reconcile Judaism and German Enlightenment values. He has fun outing the anti-Semitic subtext of nationalism, while the larger historical irony is that although Redbeard proudly displays a nationalist red-black-gold flag, the historical Barbarossa - unlike those who appropriated his image - was notably tolerant of Jews within his territories.

Appropriation, and who does it to whom, is always important in Heine. *Deutschland* shows how nationalism's appropriation of German culture and Romanticism can be opposed by being exposed as opportunistic and contradictory. It points up the clash between inclusive Enlightenment-derived civic definitions of nationality and the exclusive ethnic-organicist ones of those who, in Heine's words, 'carry only race and pure-blood and such thoughts worthy of a horse-peddler around in their heads'. For Heine, then, national unity without a liberal political-social content is a recipe for reaction. In his introduction to *Deutschland*, he anticipated his nationalist detractors:

I can already hear their beery voices: 'You blaspheme our flag, you defamer of the fatherland and friend of the French, to whom you would give up our liberated Rhine!' Calm down. I will regard and respect your flag when it deserves it, when it is no longer just an idle or a servile plaything. Hoist the red, black and gold on the heights of German thought. Make it the emblem of free humanity and I will give my heart's best blood for it …The people of Alsace Lorraine will once more join Germany if we complete what the French have begun ... if we destroy servitude everywhere, even in its last place of refuge, in heaven, if we redeem the God who dwells on earth within man, if we become God's redeemers, if we restore to dignity the poor people who have been deprived of their heritage of happiness ... Yes: then, not merely Alsace and Lorraine, but the whole of Germany will become ours, the whole of Europe, the whole world - the whole world will become German. Of this mission and the universal sovereignty of Germany I often dream when walking under oak trees. That is *my* patriotism.

Like the poem, this forces the reader to distinguish between different forms of 'Germany', pointing to the internal divisions within it as a concept. Who will any forthcoming revolution be for ? If for the aristocrats and the rich, then freedom and 'dignity' will still be denied to 'the poor people'. But if the German revolution champions universal, not just German rights, then the maiden Europa will be 'betrothed' to freedom, as envisioned in Caput 1. A German revolution will become the next stepping-stone to human emancipation.

One of the issues raised here is the question of who might lead the revolution which Heine believed, until 1848, would happen in his lifetime. In France, it had been the middle-classes. But their German counterparts, as Heine saw, were philistine, nostalgic, subservient to autocracy, and could probably not be relied upon to carry out their historical mission. Satire directed against the middle classes and liberals, as well as nationalists, is therefore also a theme. Food imagery can make the point, indicating as it does a well-fed complacency. Thus, in Caput 9, the groaning board tells of those who have kept quiet, eaten up and asked no questions: the cosy, *gemütlich* atmosphere, symbolized by the 'sincere' roast goose, tells us that these people are used to having their political goose cooked. Similarly, the cicerone in Caput 19 observes that the position of the Elector of Hannover is guaranteed not by his own strength, but by the weakness of the liberals who oppose him. This passage names names, or *a* name, and one of the most notable things about *Deutschland* is that its satire is intended to give personal offence, exercising what T. J. Reed calls a 'no-holds-barred scurrility that [was] unmatched in his day', according to a belief that '[effective satire] is the militant arm of the Enlightenment's principle of publicity, according to which nothing that is done can remain wholly unaffected once revealed to the world at large.'

Not all of the many names are those of 'real' people. One of the most appealing aspects of *Deutschland* is the way it switches between real, contemporary figures and those from German folk tale, myth, legend and history, and sometimes potently blends the two groups together (the Redbeard caputs are about a historical figure *and* his legend). Folklore was a major source of German Romanticism, in particular via *Des Knaben Wunderhorn* (1806), the famous collection edited and published by Arnim and Brentano. Despite the ironic and framing devices he often applied to it, Heine - who was a friend of the Brothers Grimm and Hans Christian Anderson - was as much of an enthusiast as any of his contemporaries. This dated, so we learn in Caput 14, from the stories told by his wet-nurse - that is, he presents the material as being mother's milk to him, or nearly. This is appropriate because it is generically fitting that in a 'Märchen' - which has the specific sense of 'fairytale', rather than simply 'tale' - the narrator should meet such figures, and in this guise they mimic, amplify, or comment on the 'real' narrative to produce a form of magic realism. Yet Heine also used the material against nationalists who had appropriated its imaginative energies and immemorial provenance to ground their political programmes in an 'essential' German spirit, or *Geist.*

Some of the cast, such as the wolves, or the *doppelgänger* axe-man in Caputs 6 and 7, or the little harpmaiden (whose 'falsetto' points to the flaw in her message), are vaguely generic. Father Rhine, in Caput 5, is more specific; the joke in his case is that the most 'Germanic' of rivers is a francophile. The treatment of the cult of the Cheruscan chieftain Hermann (Arminius) in Caput 11 shows most clearly Heine's unmasking of the ideologically motivated uses to which history was put by nationalists. The defeat of Varus' Roman legions in the Teutoberg Wald in 9 AD was being promoted as the originary moment of the nation, and the force of Heine's counterfactual history, which satirizes the present in an imagined Romanized Germany, derives from the fact that the more such heroism is asserted, the more dispiriting ought to be the contrast with the lacklustre culture of the present. This is not just amusingly deflationary, since it also highlights the constructed quality of nationalist history, particularly in the attempt to build the Hermann memorial. The nationalists aim is to fix, once and for all, the flux of national memory and identity, in order to originate an organic history of a singular German *volk*, even though, as Heine would have known, it was the recent work of designing and fundraising for the Hermann monument which had brought 9 AD to public consciousness and given it status. Like so much national-Romantic 'tradition', the nationalists' Hermann turns out to be an almost purely nineteenth century creation. This doesn't mean that

Heine fails to recognize the need to belong, or for attachment to a culture. The narrator feels his heart thump and his eyes water when he nears the border in Caput 1; he is a lover of German folklore and language; he informs Hammonia that he pines for Lower Saxony's turf-smoke and nightingales in Caput 25. None of this is merely ironic. Rather, Heine allows its strength, but suggests its conflicted nature. The narrator describes attachment as a wound in Caput 24 ('I shield / the wound from public attention'), and self-division has a pedigree in Heine's work: the narrator in *Die Bäder von Lucca / The Baths at Lucca* (1830) complains that a great rift in the world runs through the heart of the Romantic poet and that his psychic wounds are also those of the collective soul of alienated modern humanity. The poetic articulation of this wound illuminates the present stage of history, but also acts as a force pushing forward to revolution.

This sense of the poet as embodying history, and as riven by the realisation of the ideal in the form of an alienating wound which drives that progress, is evident in Caputs 6 and 7. Here, the 'new and better song' becomes a call to action, which is why the narrator tells the axeman that he appears only at those moments 'when giant sympathies' - that is, the ideals of freedom described in Caput 1 - 'germinate / in me'. It is Heine at his most Marx-like and confident; his writing itself becoming the equivalent of the axe, embodying the Hegelian dialectic in accessible form, mediating between it and the world in conveying the need for revolution, and smashing the bones of the old system. Earlier, however, we have been told of the narrator's own ripped-open breast and the dripping heart from which he takes blood to smear on door-posts in his imitation of the Passover ritual; and, as the axe comes down on the Magi, blood gushes from his breast in a flood. For Heine, the action of breaking up the old order may be necessary, but is also self-wounding, and certainly not easy or simple.

In the poem's final Hamburg section, the narrator meets the most amusing, but also the most monitory of all these legendary figures. Prior to this, the meeting with Heine's mother (in Caput legendary 20), the Hamburg townsfolk (in Caputs 21 and 22), and his publisher, Julius Campe (in Caput 23) show him thawing out a little; he shows tenderness and tact towards his mother, nostalgia and regret for beloved places and eccentric locals, many now lost or changed, and a joshing but sincere regard for Campe. Hamburg itself is the antithesis of Prussia - an independent Republic, it is also a port, and therefore outward-looking, and, unlike the Prussian garrison towns, contains a red-light district where libidinous energies may find an outlet. Hammonia, who represents both flesh and fantasy suggests that another of Heine's reasons in using such figures was to assert the rights of the imagination, fantasy and the unconscious life within politics. In the penultimate episode of *Deutschland* Heine's assault on Prussianness reaches a purgative, purgatorial crescendo in the vision the narrator is vouchsafed when he peers into Hammonia's chamberpot for a vision of the German future. This is at once an absence - he has been sworn to silence, so we learn nothing of what he sees - and a deeply prophetic stench of shit, 'rancid cabbage and Russian leather', both hilarious and shockingly void. Many have drawn the line at such scatology. Sammons has called it 'the most stupendously disgusting posture of the poet-persona to be found anywhere in Heine's writing', while Hanna Spencer claimed that 'Even devoted fans... must find these passages crude and tasteless'.

Thirty or more years on from these criticisms, it is difficult to see what the fuss was about. The poem attempts a representation of the political dunghill of the thirty-six German states; given this, an olefactory image is more pungently concise than a visual one. It is also manages to be remarkably, frighteningly prescient of Germany under the Prussians, the Nazis and the Stalinists. If the revoltingness is Augustan, the convention structuring the episode is Romantic - that to name the moment of fulfilment ironically destroys it. The sense that we are glimpsing a national unconscious is paralleled by the feeling that it is the narrator's, too: his collapse, Hammonia's attempt to seduce him, and his castration by the censor, would provide a field day for a Freudian (perhaps based on Heine's emasculating relationship to his rich relatives and his acceptance-rejection by the mother / fatherland). More to the point however is the way Heine uses ordure to subvert order, and what this says about his concept of the political in a larger sense.

This is because it is not just in the Hammonia episodes that the lower is symbolically turned against the higher. So much of *Deutschland* recalls the carnivalesque as defined by Mikhail Bakhtin in his celebrated study *Rabelais and his World*, a study which argues that the licensed foolery of the Middle Ages (fairs, carnivals, mardi gras, etc.) articulated a protest against feudal society, and that literature projected this conflict in the social body in terms of a struggle between the 'lower' and 'higher' parts of actual bodies (ie: between the stomach, genitals, anus, and their urges and functions on the one hand, and the brain and heart and their functions on the other). Such notions, like others of Bakhtin's - the double-edged subversiveness of carnival levelling, 'grotesque realism', the popular collective body - shed light on *Deutschland*. Surprisingly, given the poem's insistence on appetite and excretion, these aspects have not attracted much comment. Yet they clearly have a bearing, for example, on the banal (but exultant) imagery of food that counterpoints the socio-political narrative: garden peas, oranges, roast goose, ham omelette, roast pig, hock, sausages, boiled larks, sprats, oyster, mock turtle soup...The function of such imagery, as elsewhere in Heine, is deflationary - we are being dragged back to earth - but eating, and what it says about a culture, belongs to Heine's concern with the 'grosse Suppenfrage'. So pervasive is this imagery that it might be said to temporarily abolish within the poem a society based on want and inequality, while the plenitude within the text temporarily embodies the heaven on earth and creates the 'better song' promised in Caput 1. (In this context it is worth noting that 'Zuckererbsten für alle!' has been widespread graffito in Germany since the 1960s).

Read this way, we can see that politics in *Deutschland* exceeds what we usually think of as 'the political'. One aspect of Heine's problematic modernity lies in his conviction that we ignore our affective, somatic and irrational, unconscious selves at our peril, and that it is necessary to draw on their energies in any genuine struggle for freedom. This lies behind the mixing of literary genres and materials already discussed, and is of a piece both with Heine's homelessness and his poem's prophetic power. As J. P. Stern claims, *Deutschland* rehearses arguments from Heine's *On the History of Philosophy and Religion in Germany*, a basic premise of which is that the Germans are a people of essentially pagan energies barely modified and suppressed by a Christian veneer - first Catholicism of a flesh-denying and Devil-haunted intensity, then fervent Protestantism, finally Idealist Deism and atheism. The suppressed energies in the national psyche, for Heine, lay behind the thoroughness of the philosophical revolution of Kant, Hegel and their successors. Heine did not see this as a merely intellectual system, but rather as a living force, one that could make a German revolution universally liberating. But what if, without the final restraint of religion, and with its systematic power, the unleashed pagan forces took on a violent, reactionary aspect?

Put in less poetic terms, as an insider-outsider Heine understood that the belatedness of Germany's development played into the hands of Prussia. He could not have foreseen exactly how Germany's hothouse growth of industry, technology and science would develop from middle-class energies which could find no outlet in developing a complex civic and political life; nor could he have foreseen exactly how, as a result, politics would be dominated by the Junker autocratic caste, while dangerously vague nationalism became the substitute for middle-class participation in politics; nor how, on the back of this abnegation, would arise an 'unholy matrimony between bloodless intellectuality and bloody barbarism', in Stern's phrase, which found its incarnations in Wilhelmine and Nazi aggression. But Heine was aware of sharing the contradictory German urge to both repudiate the world and to triumph in and over it, and this gave an awesomely prophetic ring to some of his writings.

As with Nietzsche in the 1870s, his deepest anger and fear was aroused by a parvenu social formation: thus in Caput 17, Redbeard's vengeance is finally approved because his Holy Roman Empire is less dangerous than the unholy 'chivalry in spats' of Prussia, with its vicious blend of romantic concepts of the *Volk*, bureaucracy and militarism. It was this dystopian hybrid which threatened a German revolution which would not liberate mankind, but 'ravage the soil of our European life mercilessly with swords and axes':

> When you hear the thunder and crashing, you children next
> door, you French, then take care not to meddle in the work that
> we are accomplishing in Germany; or else it might be the worse
> for you… Do not laugh at the visionary who expects the same
> revolution to occur in the phenomenal realm as has happened
> in the realm of the mind… German thunder, being German, is
> not very agile and rolls along rather slowly; but it will arrive in
> due course, and when you hear such a crash as has never yet
> been heard in the history of then world, then you will know that
> German thunder has finally reached its goal…A spectacle will
> be performed in Germany, compared with which the French
> Revolution will look like a harmless idyll.

The Heine of the *History* and the Hammonia caputs properly belongs to the darker, dissident, prophetic strand of German culture which includes not only Nietzsche, but Marx, Freud, Wagner and Thomas Mann. Stern notes: '[the identification with both sides of the conflict]… is much the same… as that fought out three decades later by Nietzsche, and three decades after that by Thomas Mann in his *Meditations of a Non-Political Man*… That death-wish which Wagner dramatized and set to polyphonous music in *Tristan*; which… Freud named, and placed at the root of all devaluations of the substantial world… that death-wish Heine described in terms of *isms* and tags of philosophical argument'. E. M. Butler, despite disliking the Hammonia episodes, claimed that 'The impression [of the miasmatic odours]… is almost identical with the sensations caused by the accounts of Belsen and Buchenwald, and it needed courage to evoke them.' Even if too much has been made of Heine's clairvoyance, and the final caput looks ahead to a 'new generation' 'free of dissimulation and "sin"', this passage has enormous historical resonance.

Because of its provocative brilliance, and the rawness of the national wounds it probes, the reception of *Deutschland* has been something of a touchstone for the condition of Germany since its publication. In the nineteenth century, predictably, liberals found it difficult to defend, while right-wingers and anti-Semites found it easy to attack. Equally predictably, the poem found its chief supporters within the German Social Democratic movement, and Franz Mehring channeled this into literary criticism. In 1893, August Bebel, the leader of the party gave an address to the Reichstag on the future of socialism which concluded with the introductory lines *of Deutschland*; 1.7 million copies of Bebel's speech were subsequently distributed. Later, it was deemed so talismanic by Rosa Luxemberg and Karl Liebknecht that the Spartakist League republished it on the eve of their doomed uprising in January 1919. Yet, under the first democratic government of Germany, the Weimar Republic (1919-33), interest in Heine waned. His poetry was regarded as not being committed enough by the Left; and, of course, with the Nazis, it was swept away.

By the early twentieth century, in any case, Heine was suffering because of the rise of Modernism and a poetry which prized autonomy (something which, ironically, Heine had been one of the first to champion). Karl Kraus's 1910 essay 'Heine und die Folgen' / 'Heine and the consequences' condemned Heine's inauthentic use of language. In similar terms, the Marxist critic, Theodor Adorno, in a celebrated essay 'Heine the Wound', written some forty years later, castigated the language of the *Buch der Lieder* lyrics as not merely conventional, but commodified: 'their spontaneity was one with reification', their fluency 'derived from the language of communications'. Although Adorno's tribute to Heine is moving - 'The wound that is Heine will heal only in a society that has achieved reconciliation' - he had little knowledge of the later poetry or the *Zeitgedichte*. As Reed notes, Adorno damns with faint praise, 'tak[ing] over (rather than rebut[ting]) the anti-Semitic argument.'

The Second World War changed the reception of Heine and *Deutschland* profoundly. Like Germany itself, it split, with both poet and poem becoming Cold War trophies. Brecht wrote a party line version (mercifully a failure) in the 1940s, while the singer-poet Wolf Biermann produced a popular updating in the 1960s. *Deutschland* had the dubious fate of being universally taught and approved in the DDR as a work second only to Goethe's *Faust*, all of Heine's dubieties about 'kitchen-equality' and the 'demonic destructive power' of the masses being suppressed. In the FDR, Heine studies languished by way of reaction; in the first six years of the existence of the *Heine-Jahrbuch* (1962-67), for example, there was only one contribution from a West German professor. Complicating this attempted appropriation was Heine's Jewishness: both Germanies were keen to distinguish themselves from the Nazi regime, and as Marcel Reich-Ranicki notes, positive discussion of Heine became (and still is, to some degree) implicitly an act of anti-anti-Semitic reparation.

A story used to be told to illustrate the futility of Nazi attempts to purge German culture of its Jewish 'impurities'. The Nazis, the story ran, wanted to produce a school anthology which from which all Jewish writers had been removed. But it foundered on the realization that one of the two or three most famous poems in the language - one every German knew, the one set to music more often than any other - was Heine's 'Die Lorelei'. The poem therefore had to be included, but attributed to an 'unknown author'. There are many ways of reading this story, however; and since no confirmatory documentary evidence has ever been found, it might be argued that it was a guilty projection, in which case it symbolizes even more poignantly Heine's dual rootedness in, and inassimilability to, German literature. Since the fall of the Berlin Wall, the situation has changed again, of course; and Heine's bicentenary in 1997 saw a new complete edition of his works, along with a spate of critical studies. Even so, he still sits uncomfortably in the German literary tradition, and it has been argued by Reed that he has never really come home. But this might not be such a bad thing; the qualities which will always make Heine awkward - his libertarian politics, his Jewishness, his dual Franco-German allegiances, his 'high' and popular cultural status - these might well be seen as exemplary at the beginning of the twenty-first century. Heine was the first of those writers who can be called 'axial', negotiating as he did between different cultures, and different levels of cultures, an ironic yet hopeful bridge-builder more relevant than ever in our age of electronic interconnectedness. With this in mind, *Deutschland*'s radical, yet witty and humane advocacy of freedom, its promise of globalization from below rather than above, is supremely relevant to our own times, beset as they are also by religious bigotry, xenophobia and superpower posturing.

The text

Deutschland: Ein Wintermärchen was first published in 1844 by Hoffmann & Campe as a supplement to the *Neue Gedichte / New Poems* volume. Later in the year the poem was issued on its own, with awareness of the censors requiring a number of minor revisions.

I have worked from Barker Fairley's text of 1966, which is based on the standard editions by Elster, Walzel and Kaufmann. This has meant following the first edition rather than the second, and not restoring material from any of Heine's manuscript draft variants. Illuminating though this material is, Heine and his publisher were old hands in the game of circumventing the censors, and the few revisions which were made almost invariably resulted in a wittier and more economical version.

The effectiveness of any translation of *Deutschland* partly depends on the attitude of a translator to the technical demands of the form in which it is written. *Deutschland*'s ballad stanza is one of the staple forms of German folk poetry, and was used by Heine and his contemporaries as a way of achieving simplicity and directness. In each quatrain, the first and third lines have four iambic stresses, the second and fourth three. Like his sources, however, Heine permitted himself to use additional unstressed syllables, breaking the monotony of the iambic rhythm and giving the line more bounce. With them, the first and third lines acquire a dactylic, galloping measure and the second and fourth a trochaic, rocking one. This particular ballad form also has disyllabic end-rhyme on second and fourth lines (abcb).

Less complex than the ballad form used in poems such as Goethe's 'Die Erlkönig' or Heine's own 'Die Lorelei', the *Deutschland* ballad verse form, as Sammons has noted, lacks suppleness and, in a poem of over two thousand lines can 'threaten to rattle monotonously over long stretches.' Heine largely avoids monotony through a varied verbal texture, something which all translators must match. Apart from the usual poetic devices (alliteration, assonance, varied line length, caesura, enjambement), Heine famously taps the comic potential of disyllabic rhyme, most famously with 'Romantik' / 'Fouqué, Uhland, Tieck' in Caput 3. All previous translators of *Deutschland*, have kept these rhymes. Some, such as Margaret Armour (in her excellent but now little-known version of 1904) and Reed, have shown particular ingenuity in this regard, and both served as an inspiration, in their different ways, to my own efforts.

However, while I have remained bound, by and large, to the abcb rhyme scheme of the ballad form, respecting this basic 'home key', I have re-thought the wisdom of maintaining his disyllabic rhymes throughout. This has not been a systematic rebellion. In some places, such as Caput 11, with its rhymes on real names, matching them was not only relatively easy but artistically justifiable. But gift rhymes, or runs of easy rhymes, do not mean that such a demanding technical requirement can be fulfilled consistently without doing violence to sense or poetic fitness. As Fairley observes, the rhymes in Heine 'never, or hardly ever, obtrude themselves' - something which, unfortunately cannot be said of English translations. Soon after producing a translation of my own, in full disyllabic glory, I decided that the negative effect of the rhymes outweighed the virtues of slavish loyalty. While I remained committed to a substantial amount of *Deutschland* rhyming more or less as the original did, I ditched the principle of maintaining it at all costs and began to explore alternatives which might loosen their procrustean grip.

One problem is that there are simply fewer disyllabic rhymes in English than in German. Moreover, those that do exist are often predictable ('borrow' immediately conjures up 'sorrow' or morrow') and this diminishes the shock effect on which comic and witty rhymes depend. The paucity of rhymes also forces translators who makes a fetish of the disyllabic rhyme to use vague approximations of unconvincing coinages to meet demand. Horns become 'rousers' as surely as drinkers become 'bowsers', and readerly trust in the poem's literary quality is swiftly dissipated. This spreads to syntax and sense; inversions and distortions are demanded, items have to be differently ordered, and in some cases the original has to be dispensed with altogether. What begins as a kind of faithfulness to the original, encouraged by a few easy successes, leads to lack of accuracy and poetic failure.

By 'poetic' here I mean a function of linguistic precision, not the vaguely poetic; the closer to Heine's meaning one could manoeuvre the English, it seemed to me, the greater the chances of real poetry emerging. I decided that maximum accuracy had to be aimed at, even at the expense of the text's most obvious 'trick'. My example in this not so much earlier versions of *Deutschland* as the most recent successful translations of poems by poets (for example, Ciaran Carson's *Inferno*). The most relevant point about such translations was their use of a wide spectrum of rhyme. English language poetry of the last hundred years has compensated for lack of full rhymes by extending its franchise. From Wilfred Owen to Paul Muldoon, poets have modified our sense of what is possible in this regard. Poetry readers have been attuned to this for some time now, and are adept at responding to subtle and concealed forms of rhyme. This gives the translator an opportunity to render the original with less distortion whilst still conforming to an acceptable rhyme scheme and it seemed to me that in the case of *Deutschland*, - which is noted for its colloquial vigour and its distinctively modern tone - ignoring the current state of English poetic practice was to look an extremely rewarding gift horse in the mouth.

I have, therefore, put the tricks of modern verse-making to work, deploying pararhyme, sight rhyme, assonantal and consonantal rhyme, internal rhyme, and any other kind of rhyme, for example rhyming stressed with unstressed syllables, or Irish *deibhde* rhyme (eg: 'logíc' / 'stíck', where the rhyme syllable in 'logic' is not the one which carries the word's main stress). Sometimes I have also rhymed the first and fourth, or second and third, rather than the second and fourth lines. Very occasionally rhymes occur between stanzas. I have often used these devices as well as end-rhymes in the standard position in order to maintain a consistently rich verbal texture. Pararhyme has its own doggerel depths, of course, but I have sometimes risked falling into them in order to produce a *Deutschland* which reads convincingly as a poem in modern English. Although the aim has been to get as close to the original as possible, I have tried not to make a fetish of my own practice and forgo all of the translator's more traditional liberties. Matching 'all the tea in China' with 'finer' in Caput 26 was as hard for me to resist as it was for some earlier translators (although this is perhaps the boldest deviation from the original). More common, though still fairly rare, is a phrase like 'hypocrite lictor' in Caput 6, echoing Baudelaire's 'hypocrite lecteur'. 'Lictor' is the original, but 'hypocrite' is a blatant anachronism, since *Deutschland* predates *Les Fleurs du Mal* by thirteen years. Even so, it reproduces in English the kind of pun, usually untranslatable, which is found in the poem; and, in its defence, it is the kind of thing a *doppelgänger* or twin ('mon semblable') would say, and neatly implicates the narrator in the violence he wills (he is a sort of 'hypocrite' after all). I will leave readers to find other examples. While no guarantee of success, it is reassuring to know that this practice is endorsed Michael Hamburger, who observes that 'Where the original text is [playful] faithfulness not only permits but demands a greater measure of independence.'

Heinrich Heine

Heine was born in 1797 into a Jewish family in Düsseldorf in the liberal Rhineland province of Berg. After an unsuccessful start in business, he studied law in Bonn, Berlin and Göttingen. Between 1821 and 1823, he moved in Berlin cultural circles, attending lectures by Hegel, whose philosophy informed his political outlook. His first book, *Poems* (1822), expanded as *Book of Songs* (1827), was later to bring him fame for its romantic-ironic lyrics. For much of his life, however, Heine was better known as a prose writer, and four volumes of his ironic and often politically subversive travel-writing appeared between 1825 and 1831.

Inspired by the French Revolution of 1830, Heine moved to Paris, where he was to spend the rest of his life. In 1835, his work was branded subversive by the Federal Diet, and his writings were banned in the German Confederation. A brief friendship with Karl Marx, whom he met in Paris in 1844, influenced *Poems of the Times*, published as part of his second great poetry collection, *New Poems* (1844) which included *Germany: A Winter's Tale*.

From 1848, Heine was confined to what he called his 'mattress-grave' by a painful paralytic illness. Nevertheless his late collections, *Romanzero* (1851) and *Poems 1853 and 1854* (1854), contain some of his finest poetry. He died in Paris on 17 February 1856 and is today regarded as a key figure in the development of Romantic irony and the modern lyric, as well as an innovative master of German prose.

CAPUT 1

It was in the glum month of November,
with days growing overcast,
and the wind tearing leaves from the trees,
when I left for Germany at last;

and as I approached the border,
I felt a stronger pounding
against my ribs (I believe my eyes
even began to water);

and when I heard German spoken
I felt strange—as if, and this
is the only way I can put it—my heart
had haemorrhaged in bliss.

A little harpmaid was singing.
She sang with genuine feeling,
in a falsetto—and yet I was still
deeply moved by her keening.

She sang of love and love's sorrows,
of self-sacrifice, and of meeting
again, up in that better world
where ends all woe and grieving.

She sang of this wretched vale of tears
and of those friends, snatched too early
from us, of souls transfigured
by joy for all eternity.

She sang the old denial hymn,
the Pie-in-the-Sky-Bye-and-Bye
they croon to that dozing lout,
the People, when it stirs and cries.

But I know the tune, I know the text,
and I know all those authors—
how they secretly swig wine
while they publicly preach water.

I'll sing you a newer, better song
my friend—about how we want to build
the Kingdom of Heaven, right now,
right here, in this existing world.

We want to be happy on earth,
we won't put up with hunger—
why should the idle belly be stuffed
at the hands' expense any longer?

There's enough food for everyone—
come to that, enough roses too,
and myrtles, desire and beauty,
and, last but not least, garden peas.

Yes: sweet, juicy peas for everyone
as soon as the pea-pods split!
We'll leave Heaven for the angels
and the sparrows to inherit—

and if, after death, we still sprout wings,
we'll want to pay you visits
up there and, well, we'll dine with you
on blesséd tarts and biscuits.

So: a newer, better song—
one scored for fiddle and flute;
the miserere is outdated,
passing-bells are clappered out.

The maiden Europa is betrothed
to that good-looking genius
Freedom; they lie there, embracing,
they've indulged in their first kiss.

And if priests withold their blessing
their vows are no less valid—
long live bridegroom and bride,
and the children of their marriage!

My song's pure epithalamium—
better, newer!—and in my soul,
stars of the most exalted
consecration are ascending—

inspired stars, they go nova
blending into fiery streams—
I feel miraculous strength; I could
smash oaks into smithereens!

Since I set foot on German soil,
magic juices have coursed my veins—
the giant is earthed to his mother,
and his powers revive again.

CAPUT 2

While the little girl sang and strummed, plink-plunk,
about her longing for heaven,
the Prussians customs men
turned their attentions on my trunk.

They snuffled, rummaging through
shirts, handkerchieves, trousers;
they were looking for lace, for jewellery
and for the works of rabble-rousers.

You stupid plods, rifling my trunk!
You want an open and shut case,
but the contraband I carry
is stashed inside my brains;

and the lacework in there is finer
than any from Malines or Brussels,
and once I get my needles unpacked
I'll stitch you up a few puzzles.

The jewels I carry are all up here,
sparklers for the future's crown;
the temple treasures of a new God—
the great, the stupendous, Unknown.

And so many books are in my head!
I have to declare that it looks
just like a twittering bird's nest
of consfiscatable books.

Believe me, in Satan's own library
there can't be worse; they're even
more dangerous and devilish than those
of Hoffmann von Fallersleben!—

Then, a passenger standing next to me
broke in on my reveries.
He observed that the great Prussian
Zollverein was spread before us:

"The Zollverein", he opined,
"will *ground* the national soul—
it will take the fragmented fatherland
and bind it into a whole.

It gives us an outer unity,
that is, the so-called material sort;
while spiritual unity, the true
ideal, comes from the censor—

he gives us an inner unity,
unity of mind and of thought;
a united Germany's what we crave,
united within *and* without."

CAPUT 3

Aachen Cathedral. Charlemagne
is buried under the spire
(whatever you do, don't confuse him
with the Swabian Karl Mayer).

I wouldn't be dead, though, even for
an Emperor's alabaster;
better to *live*, if only in Stukkert-
am-Neckar as a poetaster.

At *Aaa*chen, the very dogs are bored
they fawn on you in submission—
"O stranger, give us a kick! It might
break the tedium a little ..."

And in that oh-so-boring dump
I dragged out an hour... Once more
I saw the Prussian military—
they haven't changed at all.

Still the same grey greatcoats, with
the high, red collar—('The red',
according to Körner's old song,
'means French blood has been shed').

They're still a wooden, pedantic breed,
there's still a hard right angle
in their every move, and in each face
a kind of frozen conceit.

They still walk about so stiffly—
bolt upright, starched as the washing—
as though they'd swallowed the stick
which once gave them a thrashing.

The stick has never quite vanished,
they carry it in their bones;
the cosy *Du* still reminds them
of *Er*lier forelock-touching tones.

Their long moustaches are another
of conservatism's ruses;
the pigtail that used to tickle napes
now dangles under their noses.

But let's not cavil! The new cavalry
uniform does deserve praise;
the *pickelhaube* I especially like—
a helmet impaled on its own spike—

and such a chivalric momento
of the noble, bygone, Romantic
age of Johanna von Montfaucon,
of the freemen Fouqué, Uhland, Tieck;

of the Merrie Middle Ages, too,
of noble knights and squires,
who upheld the truth in their hearts,
and their coats of arms on their rears;

it smacks of tourneys and crusades,
ladyes and pious retainers;
of the pre-print Age of Faith,
before the appearance of newspapers.

Yes, yes! the helmet I like—it shows
a most magisterial wit
(and it's a princely joke, so
we have to get the point of it)—

though I'm afraid that if a storm arose,
such a spike might chance
to attract the most modern lightning
and ruin your heads for romance ...

At Aachen, on the coaching inn crest,
that detestable bird again!
Its poisonous glare came to rest
on me like acid—prussic, Prussian.

Foul fowl, if I ever happen
to lay hands on you, just the once,
I'll rip out all your feathers
and hack off all your talons.

Then I'll stick you up on a pole
on some high, windswept hill,
and summon the Rhineland marksmen
for a game of shoot-to-kill.

Whoever blasts down the bird for me,
I'll personally sceptre and crown him—
the hero!—as "Long live the King!"
and fanfares sound out all around him.

CAPUT 4

By late evening I reached Cologne,
and heard the Rhine's soft whispering;
fanned already by a German breeze,
I felt its power to give wings—

to my appetite. I ate
a ham omelette there—rather salt
it was, though, so I was forced
to drink hock to slake my thirst.

Just like gold, the hock still glows
in a rummer of green glass;
knock back a few too many
and it's bound to tickle your nose.

Such a sweet tingling in the nose
you can't refrain, for sheer delight!
It drove me out into the echoey
alleyways and thickening night.

The stone-built houses seemed to me
to want to share the mysteries
of legends from the past, chronicled
in holy Cologne's histories.

For it was here that the Church
staged its pious carnivalesque;
here the writ of the dark men ran
whom Ulrich von Hutten sketched—

here that nuns and friars kicked up
the cancan of the Middle Ages;
here Hochstraaten, their Menzel, penned
his venomous denunciations;

here that men and books alike
were consumed by flames at the stake
(they rang bells as they were blazing
and sang *Kyrie eleison*);

and here that spite and folly mated
openly, in the very streets;
you can still tell their descendants
by their sectarian hatred.

But look! Right up there—the moon
is ghosting the colossal shell
that heaves up, diabolically black—
it's Cologne Cathedral !

This was to be the spirit's Bastille,
the Jesuitical intent
to shackle German rationality
within some monstrous cell,

until Luther arose and uttered
his terrific "Halt!"
Since tools were downed that day
nobody's been back on site.

So it's unfinished—which is good,
because in its incompletion
it commemorates German fortitude
and her protestant mission.

Still, some fools in a 'Cathedral League'
are currently trying, weakly,
to resume construction work
on their medieval keep—

please, it's a lost cause. They rattle
their little tins in vain, even accept
cash from heretics, Jews, any sect.
It's proving utterly futile.

In vain Liszt tickles the ivories
At Cathedral benefit gigs;
in vain a gifted monarch
fires off orders and decrees.

The Cathedral won't be topped out
despite the donation, gratis,
of a whole shipload of stone for it
by Swabian jackasses.

It won't be finished, for all the shrieks
of owls and ravens, those ruin-
bibbers who get their kicks
haunting old steeples and belfries.

No; the time's fast approaching, when,
instead of finishing touches,
we'll be thinking of using the space
simply for stabling horses.

"But if it's a stable", some quibble,
"what will we do with the relics
of the Three Wise Men
in their shrine in the holy chapel?"

Yet I wonder, in this day and age,
why should we even care;
the Three Wise Men from the East
can find new digs elsewhere.

Here's my advice; stick them into
those three iron cages
That've hung over Münster for ages
from Saint Lamberti's tower.

The Tailor King held court in one
flanked by his two lieutenants;
but we could easily use them
for royalty with a difference.

On the right hang, say, Balthasar
dangle Melchior on the left,
Gaspar in the middle —compare
it with how they once made shift!).

For the Holy Eastern Alliance
canonised in our own day
perhaps didn't always display
itself in a sweet and pious light;

Melchior and Balthasar may have been
blunderers, who, under duress
from the revolt of their peoples
promised constitutional redress

and then broke their word—while Gaspar,
king of the Moorish multitude,
rewarded his gullible subjects
with black ingratitude!

CAPUT 5

As I neared the Rhine Bridge,
down by the harbour quays
I glimpsed Father Rhine, flowing
freely in a moon-washed haze.

'Greetings', I hailed it, 'Father Rhine—
are you keeping in the swim?
I've often thought of you,' I chaffed,
'when I was sick for home.'

Then, from the depths, I heard
this peculiar, grieving tone
like an old man's reedy treble,
a ticklish, muted groan.

'Welcome, youngster! It's good to know
I've not been quite forgotten.
I missed you thirteen years back—and
my luck's gone from bad to rotten

since; at Biberich I choked on stone,
an awful digestion-wrecker—
though heavier on my stomach lie
the lines by Nicholas Becker.

He's hymned me as if I were
some virgin so pure, so holier-
than-thou, she'd let nobody get near
the wreath of her precious honour.

Whenever I hear his stupid chant
I feel as if I ought to uproot
my old white beard, and drown
myself in my own element!

About my so-called purity
the French are better informed;
they've mingled with me before,
my waves in their waves of victory.

It was a stupid song, as casual
as it was hurtful; a pack of lies
so witless it even had me
politically compromised—

so that now, if the French come back,
I'd blush to meet them again.
Me! who begged heaven, tears thick
in my eyes, for their return,

because I liked them so much.
Those delightful Frenchies!
Tell me, do they still sing and dance?
Do they still wear white britches?

I'd give anything to see them;
but I'm too afraid of the twitting
I'd suffer because of that ditty.
I'd be mortified with shame—

De Musset, guttersnipe of letters,
might arrive, heading a platoon,
and fire off, as the drums rat-tatted,
volleys of squibs and lampoons ...'

Thus he lamented. Poor Rhine!
Not quite sure how to mollify him
I tried a few soothing words
that ran something on these lines—

'Father Rhine, you shouldn't lose sleep
over French jibes and squibs;
they're not the same French anyway,
they've even switched their britches,

swapping white ones for red—
their buttons are a different fashion,
and they don't sing or dance either;
their heads slump in a thinking-passion,

they philosophize and talk of nothing
but Kant, Hegel and Fi*sch*te;
they smoke tobacco, swig beer,
and even play at skittles.

They're turning philistine like us,
but taking to it with their fists,
belatedly; not Voltaireans
any more, they're Hengstenbergists.

De Musset is still up to his pranks;
but there are certain ways
by which his tattling tongue
could be bridled or branked.

If he drums up a slanderous joke
fifes will shrill back our revenge;
we'll pipe back his limp heroics
in the boudoirs of *demi-mondaines.*

That's oil poured on your waters, Rhine.
Don't think of insulting songs;
you'll hear a better one before long—
farewell; we'll meet again.'

CAPUT 6

Paganini was always accompanied
by a *spiritus familiaris*—
sometimes as a dog, sometimes
in the shape of the late Georg Harris.

Napoleon saw a man in red
on the eve of every great event;
Socrates had his daimon—he wasn't
stupid, or gone in the head.

I, too, hunched over my desk
at night have glimpsed—from time
to time—an uncanny, muffled guest
who stands right behind me.

Under his cloak he'd seem to clasp
something that gleamed oddly
when it caught the light—an axe,
a headsman's axe, it seemed to me.

He was stockily built; his eyes
seemed stellar, remote, aloof.
He'd never disturb me as I wrote—
stood just a little way off.

It'd been a few years since I'd seen
this singular apparition
when, suddenly, it stood there again
in shushed, moon-brilliant Cologne.

I was wandering the alleys,
preoccupied—when, like a shadow,
he appeared on my tail. If
I stopped, he stopped too;

he'd halt, as if he were waiting.
Then, when I started, he'd make tracks,
following again; so, at last,
in the middle of the Domplatz,

I stopped—it was intolerable—
and rounded on him: "Spit it out!
What's the idea of tracking me
in the middle of the night ?

I always run into you at times
when giant sympathies germinate
in me, when my mind
is overrun with inspiration—

but your gaze is so obdurate!
Explain—what have you got hidden
under your cloak? What's that glint?
Who are you ? *What do you want?*"

He replied to my outburst, drily,
his tone a tad phlegmatic;
"Please; don't try to exorcise me;
you needn't be so emphatic,

I'm not a ghost from some past age—
nothing so surprising.
Nor am I given to rhodomondtade
or your philosophising.

My nature is simple, practical.
I'm quiet and undemonstrative,
But—*nota bene*—I act out your thoughts.
My office is executive.

It may take years, but I can't rest
until I've carried out
whatever deed you've imagined:
I'm the agent of your thought.

You're judge and jury; I'm executioner.
Slave to your whims, I'll enforce
judgements you happen to pass,
however unjust, however harsh.

Roman consuls were preceded
by axe-bundles when they headed
processions—you have your *fasces* too,
but this axe brings up the rear.

So, no hypocrite lictor, I pace
unweariedly behind you:
I'm your hatchet man—the deed
to which your thought has bound you."

CAPUT 7

I went to my room and slept as if
by all the angels rocked.
You slumber best on German beds
because they're feather-flocked—

how often I yearn for the softness
of down beds, fatherland-style,
when I stretch out on the insomniac
iron mattresses of exile!

You sleep soundly, you dream well
patriotically featherbedded...
The binding chains of earth dissolve—
a German soul grows lightheaded;

and to the highest courts of heaven
the soul, unfettered, climbs.
O German soul, how proudly
you soar in your nightly dreams!

The Gods grow pale at your approach—
many of the less distinguished
stars flicker in your wing-beats' draught,
or are summarily extinguished.

France and Russia may rule by land,
Britain may rule the seven seas—
but dreamland's cloud-kingdoms
are our indisputable territories.

We exercise hegemony there;
disunity on earth doesn't matter.
The other nations all seem
products of an earth that's flatter.

As I dropped off, I dreamt
that once again I sauntered
through the moonlit, echoing alleys
of Cologne's medieval quarter.

Behind me (again!) there stalked
my muffled, dark attendant.
I was bent with exhaustion
yet on and on we walked,

we kept right on. My heart within
my breast was yawning, as if ripped,
and forth from out the heart-wound
the red drops wept and dripped.

Occasionally, I dipped a finger in,
and occasionally it happened
that as we passed a doorpost
I'd smear it with the gore—

and every time, if a house
was marked out in this manner,
I'd hear a passing-bell's distant
melancholy, its faint clangour.

But above, the moon grew fainter,
as it became more shrouded;
like black horses racing past her
she was occluded by wild clouds.

And, as ever, *he* lurked behind
clutching his hidden axe,
that figure in black. We wandered
for another long, long while—

traipsed and traipsed, until we found
ourselves in Cathedral Square again.
The cathedral doors were open wide
and we passed between them.

In the vastness nothing reigned
but death and night and silence;
here and there lamps smouldered
to make the darkness visible.

A long time I walked by the pillars
and heard nothing—nothing except
my pacing shadow; even there
he matched me step for step.

At last, we came to a place
where candlelight gulped and shone
on fiery brilliants and gold—
the Chapel of the Three Wise Men.

But its moribund inhabitants
who lie there undisturbed—
A wonder! They now sat perched
upright on their sarcophagi—

Three skeletons, fantastically arrayed,
crowns set on their yellow
pathetic skulls, each one clutching
a sceptre in his bony claw.

Like jack-in-the-boxes their long-dead bones
moved in ghastly motion;
from them rose a pungent cloud
of incense and putrefaction.

One even began working his rictus
and delivered a speech, a long one;
he told me my place, told me too
that I should respect his station—

first, because he was deceased;
second, because he was a king;
and third, because he was holy—
none of which really convinced me.

I answered, confidently smiling:
'You've completely overstated
your case; you're superannuated
in just about every way—

Begone! Clear out! The deep grave
is the best place for your chatter!
Life now stakes its claim on you
and the treasures of this chapel.

The future's rejoicing cavalry
will be stabled in this cathedral;
and if you don't leave I'll use force,
I'll let you taste their rifle-butts."

So I spoke—and, as I turned back,
I caught the terrible glitter
on my silent companion's axe;
he had certainly caught my drift.

He closed right in, and with his axe
smashed those poor skeletons
of superstition, hacking
them down without remorse.

The blows' echoes resounded,
appallingly, from the vault—
blood spurted from my breast
and I suddenly awoke.

CAPUT 8

The mail-coach to Hagen from Cologne
cost five thalers six groschen
but it was full; I had to take
the open trailer-coach.

A late autumn morning, raw and grey,
the team panted through the mire;
but despite the weather, the foul ways,
I was filled with content. Why ?

Because it was a native wind
to which my cheeks bore witness;
the country roads were the clabbery mess
of my own dear fatherland!

The team swished their tails with happiness,
like old acquaintances; their dung-
cakes shone as bright in my eyes
as Atalanta's golden apples

all the way to Mülheim—clean, placid,
a proper picture-book town.
Prosperous, too. Last time I was here
was in May of '31.

It was blossom-time then—
it was sunlight, it was birds singing
all day long; a whole population
longing, longing and thinking:

"We'll ride our skinflint lordships
out of town instanter—we'll give
them one for the road from these
special thin steel decanters—

and Freedom will dance and cavort
decked out in the red, blue and white.
Perhaps she'll even resurrect
the mortal remains of Bonaparte."

Yet the nobles are still entrenched;
most of the awful dunces
who slunk back skinny as scarecrows
have now developed paunches;

the pallid *canaille* who struck up
Faith, Hope and Charity poses
got sozzled on the Rhenish
and now sport strawberry noses.

Freedom's twisted her ankle, too,
and she can't pirouette or twist.
From spires in Paris the tricolour
droops, hangdog, at half-mast.

The Emperor was reanimated,
but the English worms preferred
a meeker, a *graver* man—
and they had him reinterred.

I myself saw the golden hearse,
the funeral obsequies;
the casque, chased and embossed
with Goddesses of Victories.

Along the Champs Elysées, threading
the Arc de Triomphe—
through fog, slush, snow, sleet and ice
the cortège slowly tramped,

the music all discords,
the musicians' sad bleatings
cramped by cold. The standard eagles
gazed in woebegone greeting

while we looked on, ghost-ridden,
overwhelmed by memories—
the fairytale Imperial dream
flickered, conjured up once more.

That day I wept; the tears welled
from my eyes as I heard
ring out the ancient, mislaid
love-cry: "Vive l'Empereur!"

CAPUT 9

At a quarter to eight that morning
I'd set out from Cologne;
we made Hagen not much before three,
though we'd been due to eat at noon.

The table was set. They'd laid on
traditional German dishes.
Greetings, my dear sauerkraut—
your aroma is so delicious!

Pickled chestnuts in green cabbage,
exactly as made by my mother!
Greetings, cod of my homeland—you swim
so cleverly in your butter!

Every sensitive heart will hold
its fatherland dear forever—
for myself, well, I'm also fond
of well-braised eggs and herring.

How the sausages sang in their spitting fat!
And the fieldfares set before us,
such pious cherubs in apple sauce,
twittered "Welcome!" in a chorus.

"Welcome, countryman," they twittered,
"we thought you'd gone forever
to wander in foreign lands with
birds of a foreign feather."

A roast goose sat on the table,
a quiet, comfortable being.
Perhaps she'd doted on me years back
when both of us were young.

She cast me such a meaning look,
so sad, so deep, so from-the-roots;
she had a beautiful soul, for sure,
but her flesh was as tough as old boots.

Also, a pig's head was borne in
on a pewter platter; as always
among us, I saw they'd decked the snout
of some old swine with the laurels.

CAPUT 10

After Hagen the night came on,
and I felt in my innards
an answering chill. I couldn't warm up
until we got to an inn in Unna.

There was a pretty barmaid there;
smiling, she ladled out hot punch.
Her eyes were soft as moonshine,
her hair was in yellow silk bunches,

and that lisping Wethtphalian accent!
It affects me like no other;
the hot punch fumed with memories,
took me back to the dear brotherhood—

the Westphalian Club—with whom
I used to drink in Göttingen.
How we sank into each others' hearts;
how we sank beneath the benches ...

No, I've always loved Westphalians—
affection isn't hard to muster
for a people so steadfast and true,
so free of bombast or bluster.

How well they'd shape up to duel,
all lionhearted! Fair, though fierce,
their manly strokes fell bluff and true—
the quarter-blow! The tierce!

They fight hard and drink deep;
when they offer a hand, they're gentle.
They shake for friendship, then blubber—
hearts of oak, but sentimental.

Heaven preserve you and your crops
you worthy race of stoics,
and keep you from war and glory,
from heroes and heroics.

May all your sons turn up to sit
the easiest of exams; and
all your daughters blush prettily
under the wedding-veil. –Amen!

CAPUT 11

This is the Teutoberg Forest—
Tacitus alludes to the region.
It's the classical morass
where Varus got stuck with his legions

and got stuck into the Cheruscan chief,
the noble warrior Herman—
though the nationality that emerged
from this foul gunge was German.

Yet if Herman and his blond hordes
hadn't won that battle
we wouldn't have German liberty now;
we'd all be Roman chattels.

Our fatherland's mother-tongue'd be Latin;
we'd wear togas instead tunics ;
Swabians would be *quirities*,
there'd even be Vestals in Munich.

Hengstenberg would be a *haruspex*
burbling his ruminations
over ox guts; while Neander, an *augur*,
would observe the birds' migrations.

Like some of the Roman ladies,
Birch-Pfeiffer would be a fanatic
for turpentine (it's said they drank it
to make their urine aromatic).

Raumer wouldn't be a German clot,
he'd be a Roman, Clotius;
Freiligrath would spout unrhymed verse,
as did Flaccus Horatius.

That great scrounger, Father Jahn,
would be named Painintheanus.
Me hercule! Latin-tongued Massmann
as Marcus Tullius Massmanus!

Truth's champions would now combat
the lion, hyena and jackal
in the arena, instead of having
gutter press newshounds to tackle,

We'd have only *one* Nero now,
Instead of the current thirty-six
princelings; to defy tyranny
and slavery we'd slit our wrists.

Schelling would be just like Seneca,
and we would offer this dictum
to our friend with the oils, Cornelius—
cacatum non est pictum.

But Herman (thanks be!) won the day.
The Romans were driven from the field.
Varus fell with his legionaries;
we stayed German; we didn't yield.

We stay German, we speak German,
because they couldn't undermine us.
A Swabian is a Swabian still;
an ass is an ass, not *asinus.*

Raumer is still a German clot—
he picked up a medal by way of reward.
Freiligrath's doggerel still rhymes;
he's no Horace, and we're still bored.

Massman, glad to say, is Latinless.
Birch-Pfeiffer sticks to dramas
and doesn't swig turpentine
like those amorous Roman mamas.

O Herman! We've you to thank for this!
So at Detmold, as is proper
they're building you a monument—
and I've chipped in a few coppers.

CAPUT 12

We lumbered through woods at night
in the chaise. Suddenly a bolt
shears, we've shed a wheel
and lurched, shuddering, to a halt.

It's no joke! The postillion
jumps down and scurries off
to the next hamlet. My heart sinks—
all alone; night, in a forest.

Then—slowly—howling, all around.
Just a pack of wolves, I thought ...
Wolves! Those famished outcries!
Eyes, yellow in the shadows!

And yet (I told myself) they know
it's me who's here; they've formed up
to honour me with torches
and a choral performance.

Yes—that's it!—a serenade.
I'm being fêted... I rose,
coughed apologetically;
gesticulated, struck the pose.

"Fellow wolves! I'm sensible
of this honour; to be here tonight,
to hear so many noble souls
lovingly howl and cry—

let me say, right now, I'm moved.
Words can't express—I'm overcome—
Friends! This hour will live with me
until the race of my life is run.

I thank you for the confidence
with which you've honoured me;
just as, in days gone by,
you proved your loyalty

fellow wolves! You never doubted!
You refused to be persuaded
by those who said I'd gone to the dogs,
that my will had been eroded,

or that I was a turncoat who'd
sought high office among the lambs
(it was beneath my dignity,
of course, to deny those claims).

The sheep's clothing I affected
was purely for insulation.
Believe me, I never lost sheep—sleep
I mean, over the ovine situation.

I'm not a sheep, dog, councillor
or haddock; I'm not some dull fish—
I've always been wolf. My heart,
my very teeth are wolfish.

Yes—I'm a wolf and I'll always
howl along with the wolves.
So count on me; and remember,
God helps those who help themselves."

Such was the address I delivered
extempore. You'll find a version
in the latest *Allgemeine Zeitung,*
mangled by Kolb's revision.

CAPUT 13

The sun came up near Paderborn
with a shrug of exasperation;
what a thankless task he has,
the stupid earth's illumination!

He lights one hemisphere, and he's
just bringing, at dazzling speed,
light to the second, when the first
darkens again on the further side.

Sisyphus's boulder rolls downhill
again; the Danaids' tun can never
be filled, and the sun tries to light
the whole globe, in vain, for ever!—

and as the morning mists dispersed
in red-streaked dawn, by the side
of the road I saw a image
of that man who was crucified.

It fills me with sorrow every time
I see you, poor cousin; why,
you wanted to redeem the world,
you fool, you saviour of mankind!

The played a vile trick on you,
the gentlemen who sealed your fate;
who told you to speak so incautiously
on questions of Church and State?

It's a misfortune that in your day
publishing wasn't an option;
in our times, you'd write *Towards
Understanding the Heaven Question*

The censor would just excise the bits
with an earthly application;
his crippling caress would thereby
have saved you from crucifixion.

Oh, if only, for the Sermon on the Mount,
you'd chosen another text;
you had brains and talent, you knew
how the pious would be vexed.

Whip-wielding, you scourged the bankers
and money-changers from the Temple,
hapless fanatic; now you're strung up there,
to serve us as an example.

CAPUT 14

Clammy wind, bleak terrain,
the chaise slogging through mud;
but this sings and rings in my head—
Sun, you accusing flame!

It was the refrain of an old song
my wet-nurse used to croon—
Sun, you accusing flame! It rang
clear as a hunting horn.

The song's about a murderer
who enjoys his liberty
until he's discovered in the forest
strung up from a willow tree.

The death sentence is hammered
into the tree's grey trunk;
it's been arrived at by the lynch mob—
Sun, you accusing flame!

The sun was the accuser. It demanded
vengeance for the crime;
Ottilie, dying, had gasped out,
"Sun—you accusing flame!"

As I think of the song, I also think
of my nurse, that dear woman;
again I see her weathered face,
with all its folds and wrinkles.

She was born in the Münster Land
and had a memory chock-full
of folk stories, ghost- and horror-tales
of monsters and the supernatural.

How my heart would pound, as the old girl
told the tale of the King's daughter
who use to sit all alone on the moor,
combing out her shiny, gold hair.

She had to tend the geese there—
she was a goosegirl, now—and each
evening she drove them through the gate,
and stood, sadly, underneath.

For nailed up on the arch, she saw
the head of a horse; the poor,
decapitated horse, that had
brought her to that far-off land.

The King's daughter sighed so deep:
"O, Falada, to see you on show!"
The horse's head cried back to her:
"O woe! that you pass below!"

The King's daughter sighed so deep:
"If only my mother knew!"
The horse's head cried back to her;
"Her heart would break in two!"

With bated breath I listened then
as my nurse, in a grave murmur
began to talk about Redbeard,
about our secret Emperor.

She assured me that he wasn't dead
as scholars might assert.
He was hiding, under a mountain,
with his army, ready to return.

The mountain's name is Kyffhäuser,
and inside it's all hollowed out;
lamps cast an eerie light
through its high-chambered halls.

The royal stables fill one vault:
there, thousands of horses
stand (each bright-harnessed
and serviceable) in their stalls.

They're all saddled and bridled,
but though in fine fettle
not one neighs, or paws, or stamps:
they stand as if cast in metal.

In the second vault, in scattered straw,
you can see the soldiers lying—
a bearded nation of thousands,
faces warlike, defiant.

Each is armed all *cap-à-pé*.
Yet not one of these brave hearts
ever so much as stirs;
they're sunk too deep in sleep.

Heaped up in the third vault
is their gear—axes, pikes, broadswords,
armour, steel casques, helms of silver,
old Frankish culverins.

Just a few cannon—yet enough, all told,
to melt down into trophies.
Projecting up from behind these
is a banner in black, red and gold.

In the fourth hall is the Emperor
himself. For ages he's dozed
in a stone throne—head in the crook
of his arm, slumped on a table of rock—

so that, by now, his red beard reaches
the floor. An eyelid twitches
sometimes; sometimes his eyebrows
may rise, his brows knit or unknit—

is he asleep, or is he thinking?
It's impossible to tell—
but when the fated hour strikes
he'll stir, they say, vigour swelling,

and grab the good old flag, and yell;
"To horse! To horse!" A clashing
will fill the vaults, they'll echo
to frantic preparations;

the troops will leap up on horses
that stamp and champ at the bit,
then charge out into the clattering world,
fanfaring till their trumpets split.

They'll ride well, and they'll fight well,
they'll have slept their due slumber.
The Emperor's judgement will fall
sternly on every murderer—

on the filthy murderers who slew
our dearest, our most miraculous
gold-tressed maid Germania—
Sun, you accusing flame!

Not one who thought himself safe,
who laughed from his castle—no bosses
or lords—will escape the noose-
justice of Barbarossa.

How lovely they sound, music to my ears,
my old nurse's fairytales!
My superstitious heart exults—
Sun, you accusing flame!

CAPUT 15

A fine, freezing rain is tingling
like ice-cold pins and needles.
The horses are sweating through the mire,
their tails glumly swinging.

The postillion blows on his horn,
I recognise the old melody—
'Three Riders Gallop Through The Gate'—
the twilight is stealing over me;

I rock and drowse, and I doze off—
and behold! Suddenly, unbidden,
I dream I'm under the mountain again
where Barbarossa is hidden.

He wasn't sitting motionless
like a statue, at a stone table;
nor could you say he resembled
the imposing figure of fable.

He was waddling through the halls with me
engaged in friendly chatter;
like an antiquarian he showed off
his curios and treasures.

In the Weapons Hall he explained
how a mace should be hefted;
he rubbed the rust off a sheaf of swords
using his cloak (it was ermine-lined).

He grabbed a bunch of peacock-feathers
to shoo the dust away
from all the harnesses and helms,
and the *pickelhaubes* too.

In the same way, he dusted off his flag.
"My greatest pride", he said,
"is that moths haven't eaten the silk—
and worms haven't been at the wood."

And when we entered the chamber
where thousands of warriors
all armoured, lie stretched in slumber,
the old man spoke with pleasure:

"We must keep quiet and go carefully,
I don't want these men to wake;
another hundred years have passed
and they get paid today."

And behold! As we passed the soldiers
the Emperor took out a ducat
as we neared each one, and gingerly
he slipped it into his pocket.

Smiling, he turned and spoke to me
as I looked on in astonishment;
"I pay each man a ducat apiece,
and I pay him once a century."

In the hall where the horses stood
in column by silent column
the Kaiser rubbed his hands in glee
(he seemed utterly unsolemn).

He counted the nags off, one by one,
smacking them on their ribs—
he counted and counted, in anxious haste
silently working his lips.

"They're still not up to full strength ,"
he said at last, slightly peeved—
"I've got plenty of weapons and soldiers—
but I'm still short of a few steeds."

"I've sent out grooms to travel
the outside world, and buy
me the best horses available—
we've amassed a pretty good total.

I'll wait until I've a full complement,
then I'll strike the blow and set free
my fatherland, my German people,
who loyally wait for me."

So said the Emperor, but I exclaimed:
"Strike the blow now, old friend,
strike—if you don't have the horses,
just take some donkeys instead."

Redbeard answered, laughing: "No need
to rush in landing the blow,
Rome wasn't built in a day, and all
good things come by degrees, you know.

Slowly but surely grows the oak,
who's not home this day will be home
the next, and *chi va piano va sano*
as the proverb runs in Rome."

CAPUT 16

The coach gave a jolt. I was awake,
but my eyelids soon drooped;
I drifted off to sleep, and began
to dream of Redbeard again.

This time I was strolling with him
through his echoing caverns;
he asked me this, he asked me that—
greedy for some answers

He'd heard nothing of the world
for many a long year
(he hadn't received any news at all
since the Seven Years War).

He asked after Moses Mendelssohn
and Karschin; displayed interest
in the affairs of Countess du Barry,
Louis the Fifteenth's mistress.

So I said, "Kaiser, you've lost touch.
Louis' long dead, as is old Moses.
Likewise his Rebecca. Abraham,
their son, is pushing up the daisies;

though Abraham, and a Leah, begot
a lad called Felix who passes muster
in christendom; he's made it
as a kapellenmeister.

Not only is old Karschin gone,
but so is her daughter, Klenke;
though her grand-daughter Helmine
Chezy's still with us—I think.

While Louis ruled the roost, of course,
du Barry strutted and preened—
that's the Fifteenth—but she was
getting on by the time she was guillotined.

Louis the Fifteenth had passed away
in bed, as *per etiquette*.
The Sixteenth, however, was guillotined
with his queen, Marie Antoinette.

The queen showed enormous courage;
her conduct didn't demean her.
But, when it came to du Barry,
she blubbered on the guillotine ..."

At which the Kaiser stopped short.
He fixed me with a stony look
and demanded "By all that's holy,
what is this, this—'guillotined'?"

"Being guillotined," I answered
"is simply the latest process
which, whatever your status,
will conduct you from life to death.

The new procedure relies
on a spanking brand-new device
patented by one Monsieur Guillotin—
hence the name, 'guillotine.'

You're strapped to a swivel plank
which seesaws smoothly in between
two posts; above, in the frame,
hangs a triangular blade.

A cord jerks a peg out—the blade falls,
whoosh!—a swift severing,
and you've lost your head forever!
A collection sack is placed just under the ..."

"*Silence*!" bellowed Redbeard,
"I won't hear another word
about this contraption! God forbid
I should ever use such a thing ...

Strapped? To a plank, you say?
The monarch and his queen?
But—but—it violates decorum!
It's utterly *obscene*!

Who are you, for that matter,
to address a king so familiarly?
Wait there, sirrah! I'll clip
your wings for such audacity.

It cuts me to the very quick
to hear what you have to say—
your merest breath is treason,
it reeks of *lèsé-majesté*!"

At this tongue-lashing I snapped—
I just had to interrupt him.
With a shout, venting my passions,
my inner thoughts erupted—

"Herr Redbeard," I almost raved,
"you're just a creature of fable—
go back to sleep! We'll save
ourselves without your help.

The republicans would laugh at us
anyway, if we were seen
led by a ghost with a crown and a sceptre,
we'd become a comic routine.

And, come to think of it, I don't hold
with your flag—not since the time
I was in the Burstenschaft myself.
It spoilt my taste for black-red-gold.

It would be best if you stayed
put under old Kyffhäuser.
I've just re-examined this subject
and concluded we don't need a Kaiser."

CAPUT 17

So I wrangled with the Emperor
in dream, in a dream; one minces
one's words in waking hours
with such contradictory princes

(only dreaming, in ideal dreams,
will a German dare assert
his German beliefs; at other times
they're buried in his loyal heart).

When I woke we were passing
through a wood. The sight of trees
in their naked, wooden reality
scattered all my dreams.

Oak trees gravely shook their heads.
Twiggy birches were looking
down sternly. "O Kaiser", I cried,
"forgive the liberties I took!

Redbeard, forgive my rash words!
I know that you're far wiser
than me; I have so little patience.
Come soon, after all, my Kaiser.

Stick to your old expedients
if the guillotine shocks you;
sword for the lords, a rope for burghers—
and peasants in their smocks, too.

Just vary things a little—let
nobles tread the air sometimes; treat
the odd serf to a blade (nowadays
we all count as God's creatures).

Restore Charles the Fifth's Star Chamber
and his penal regulations;
divide the people up again
into guilds, estates, corporations.

Restore the Holy Roman Empire
in its entirety; give us back
its putrefied gangrenous rubbish
and septic bric-à-brac.

I'd even accept the Middle Ages
and all they meant; I'd swallow
them whole to be rid of the mongrel
mish-mash in which we wallow,

this hotchpotch chivalry-in-spats,
this nauseous bastard dish
of Gothic frenzy and modern lies
that's foul, but neither flesh nor fish,

close down the theatres where the past
is parodied, and drive out
the rabble of clowns who stage it—
but just come *soon*, O Kaiser!"

CAPUT 18

A safe stronghold our Minden is still,
it has good shields and weapons;
but Prussian forts, it so happens,
always give me the shivers.

We arrived there at evening.
The planks of the drawbridge moaned
spine-chillingly as we rolled across;
the dark moat yawned below.

The bastions overlooked us
with a kind of sullen menace.
Rattling, the portcullis rose;
then, rattling, closed the entrance.

O my spirits sank at that—
just as Odysseus's sank when
Polyphemus rolled the boulder
across the mouth of his den.

A corporal met the coach and asked
for our names: all defiance
I thought: "I'm Herr No-one, oculist,
a cataract-cutter to giants!"

But I felt queasy in the tavern
and the food was unimpressive,
so I turned in. I couldn't sleep;
the bedclothes' weight was oppressive.

I'd been given a vast featherbed
curtained with red damask,
the canopy in grubby gold trim,
was topped by a filthy tassel.

That loathsome tassle! It robbed me
of sleep all night long.
Over my head it seemed to hang
like the sword of Damocles.

At times it looked like a serpent's head
which would start to hiss,
"You'll never esscape! You're sstuck
for keepss in this fortresss!"

"O that I were home again," I groaned,
"I'd give anything to not be here—
To be back in Paris with my wife,
in the Faubourg-Poissonière!"

Gradually, my thoughts iced over.
Occasionally a horrid
chill, like the palm of the censor,
passed clammily across my forehead.

Gendarmes wrapped in winding-sheets—
a ghostly chorus-line—wrangled
around my bed; from far off I heard
uncanny fetters jangled.

Ah! those spectres haled me off!
I discovered myself at last
dangling on some sheer precipice;
there they attached me fast.

That evil bed-canopy tassle!
It returned again, just as before,
but this time as a vulture—
black-plumaged and with claws,

in the form of a Prussian eagle.
It clutched my trussed-up body,
gobbling the liver from my breast
as I screamed and howled.

I howled so long—then a cock crowed,
dispelling the feverish dream.
I lay on a sweaty bed in Minden,
the eagle was a tassle again.

I pressed on by the swiftest coach,
breathing freely for the first
time only in the open country
in the vicinity of Bückeburg.

CAPUT 19

Danton, you were wrong (and you paid
for being so self-deceiving);
you can take your homeland with you
on your boot-soles as you leave it—

half the Princedom of Bückeburg
adhered, with gunky persistence,
to my boots, thanks to the worst roads
I've met in my whole existence.

I'd stopped off in Bückeburg, where
my granddad was born (I had to pay
some dues to ancestry—grand-
mother was from Hamburg, by the way),

but made Hanover by noon
and had my boots scraped well.
I set off at once to see the town—
I like getting the most from travel—

and it was so incredibly clean!
No horse-dung littering the alleys,
loads of marvellous buildings,
impressively bulky, really—

I liked, especially, one grand square
formed by mansions—grand, dutiful-
looking—and a palace where the King lives,
whose exterior is quite beautiful

(the palace's, that is). At its gate,
guarding the main entrance—
muskets shouldered, at attention—
were two fierce, red-coated sentries.

"Ernst Augustus's place" my cicerone
observed, "an old Lord, and a rank Tory,
but vigorous for his age",
he added. "Although the real story

is his absolute safety, which, much more
than the henchmen round his throne,
is protected by our good friends'
Liberal lack of stiff upper lips.

I see him sometimes; he complains
of the boredom of his position
as king; says that in Hanover he's
quite *condemned* to his royal station;

that, compared with English society,
life's too straitened; that the spleen
plagues him till he almost fears
he'll hang himself from sheer ennui.

The other day, in the small hours,
I found him bent by the fire. Sad—
with his own hands he'd brewed an enema
for a dog that was feeling bad."

CAPUT 20

From Harburg it was an hour's ride
to Hamburg. A soft evening;
stars mellowed the winter skies,
the breeze was sweet and soothing

and when I came to my mother's
she just shrieked for joy. She cried
and cried "My dear child!", beating
and wringing her hands together.

"My *dear* child! Thirteen years
it's been since we last met!
You must be absolutely ravenous!
Tell me; what would you like to eat?

I've got fish and some roast goose
and some beautiful oranges—"
"Well! give me fish and goose then
Mama—and the beautiful oranges."

As I started on the first dish
my mother hovered by, beside
herself ; enquiring about this—
and about that, and the other.

"Dear child! Are you treated
well abroad? Is your wife any good
at housekeeping? Can she darn neatly?
Can she patch your shirts?"

"Mama; the fish is perfect, but
it's rude to talk with your mouth full,
and so easy to choke on a bone.
You mustn't disturb me just yet."

After I finished the worthy fish
the goose was carried in.
Again Mama asked about that and this,
with the occasional tricky question.

"Dear child! In what country
do they lead the best existence?
Here, or in France? And which
nationality do you like best?"

"Dear Mama; the German goose is
good, and yet the French
stuff their geese better than we do.
They also have better sauces."

After I'd demolished the goose
and its carcase made its exit
the oranges came. They gushed
with juice—well worth the wait—

but yet again my mother began
her awkward questions; she touched on
a thousand different subjects. Some
were pretty close to the bone.

"Dear child! A penny for your thoughts—
is your hobby still politics?
Is there any party to which
you would lend your support?"

"The oranges, Mamma, are so sweet
and full of juice they're incredible.
I've sucked them dry, but I've left
the peel. It's inedible."

CAPUT 21

In the city's burnt-down quarters,
rebuilding had just started.
Like a poodle that's been half-shorn
Hamburg looks quite martyred.

Many streets were lost to me,
losses I could only grieve—
where's that house where I stole
my very first kisses of love?

Where's the printshop where I saw
Travel Sketches from the presses?
Where's the oyster cellar where
I swallowed my first oysters?

And the Dreckwall, where has the Dreckwall gone?
I'd look for it now in vain.
Where is the pavilion,
where I devoured so many cakes?

Where's the Town Hall, where the senate
and the City Council were throned?
Spoils of the fire! Not even that
holiest of holies remains.
.
The people sigh; they're still shaken.
With an anxious, crestfallen air
they regaled me with appalling
tales of the conflagration.

"It flared up in every district at once!
Nothing but smoke and flames all around;
the church towers just blazed up,
imploded and came crashing down.

The Bourse, where our forefathers
dealt for a century with each other
as honestly as they possibly could—
the old Bourse is completely gutted.

Though the Bank—the city's silver soul—
and its ledgers, which held records
of every man's cash value, was
(praise be to God!) spared to us.

Praise be! A disaster appeal
was organized abroad—a brilliant
business, that—and it raised
getting on for eight million.

Money flowed from all nations
into our open hands;
they sent us victuals too—we didn't
spurn any contributions.

We were sent loads of clothes and bedding—
also bread, meat and soup;
the King of Prussia even wanted
to donate some of his troops.

The material damage was restored—
according to our calculations.
But as for the fright, the alarm we had,
nothing could compensate us."

I tried to cheer them: "Good people,
do stop harping on your trouble;
Troy was a greater city than yours
but it was reduced to rubble.

Rebuild your houses. Wipe your noses.
Dry your eyes and drain the puddles.
Sort out the insurance muddles,
and invest in more fire-hoses.

Don't fling pimento-cayenne
on your mock-turtle soup so madly
in future ; and don't eat carp
covered in scales and fried in lard.

Turkeys won't do you too much harm,
but do beware of nastier
birds—the kind that's laid its egg
in the wig of your *Bürgermeister.*

I'm sure you don't need telling
the name of this deadly bird;
simply thinking about the word
sets the food churning in my belly."

CAPUT 22

Even more changed than the city
are its inhabitants. They ramble
the streets sadly, broken; ruins
on legs, threatening to tumble.

Those who were slim are skeletal,
the plump are fatter; children seem old
while the old seem infantilised,
as if in a second childhood.

Many I left behind as calves
have turned out oxen; several puny
goslings have grown up to be geese
and cackle, proud of their plumage.

I found old Gudel pancake-faced
and tricked out like a Siren (she's
acquired raven tresses somehow
and a set of white, dazzling teeth).

Best-preserved of all was my friend
the paper merchant; hair wrapped his
head like the yellow nimbus
in a portrait of John the Baptist.

As for Halle, I managed to see
him from a distance—he avoided me.
I heard his mind was burnt out, but
that it had been insured with Bieber.

And I saw my old censor again;
fog-environed, head bowed low,
he bore down on me in the Goose Fair.
He seemed bent double by his woes.

We shook hands; and in the eyes
of this man, of all men, tears swam;
he was "overjoyed" to see me again—
what a heartwarming scene!

I didn't find them all. Many had
died in the years I'd been away.
My Gumpelino, I'm afraid,
is one I'll never meet again;

that noble man had recently breathed
his last, his great soul passing over;
he'll be a transfigured seraph now
at the mercy-seat of Jehovah.

And I looked everywhere, in vain,
for the crooked Adonis who hawked
china cups and chamberpots
in the alleyways and courts.

Sarras, that loyal hound, is dead.
A terrible loss! I'll wager
Campe would rather have lost
a whole pack of his writers.

The city of Hamburg's populace
has consisted, time out of mind,
of Jews and Christians; the latter. I'd add,
aren't know for their extravagance.

For the Christians are all pretty virtuous;
they also eat heartily at noon, and
they promptly honour bills of exchange—
or at least before the final demands.

The Jews split into two different
parties. The division is simple—
old Jews go to the synagogue,
the new Jews go to the temple.

The new Jews eat pork, are
bloody-minded, refractory
and democrats; while the old
are much more *aristoscratchy*.

I love the old and I love the new—
but I swear by the living God that
I love certain fishes even more,
the kind that are known as smoked sprats.

CAPUT 23

As a republic, Hamburg was never
on a par with Venice or Florence.
But it does the best oysters. You get
the finest at the *Keller Lorenz.*

It was a glorious evening when I
proceeded there with Campe;
we were planning to pamper
ourselves with Rhenish and oysters—

and the company was good enough.
I was glad to meet old friends—
Chaufepié, for example—and
more recent brothers of the pen.

Wille was there; a man whose face
is marked, like a palimpsest
which his enemies, in his student days,
have so legibly impressed;

Fuchs, too, a benighted heathen
and personal foe of Jehovah
(he only believes in Hegel, and maybe
the Venus of Canova).

My Campe played Amphitryo.
He beamed with joy. He grinned,
eyes wide with bliss—like a picture,
he was, of the Blessed Virgin.

There I was, feasting heartily,
thinking as I mellowed
"This Campe is a paragon
of publishers, a capital fellow!

Other publishers, maybe,
would have left me to go hungry—
but this one even stands me drinks:
I'll never abandon him.

Thanks be to the Creator on high
who created the juice of the vine,
and who, out of all the publishers,
made Julius Campe mine.

Thanks be to the Creator on high,
who, by his mighty Let-There-Bes,
fashioned the oyster-crowded seas
and planted the grapes by the Rhine—

Who let the very lemons we squeeze
on oysters be manifested—
and now, Heavenly Father, just grant
a night of sound digestion!"

Rhenish always gets me this way:
it converts strife to unanimity
in my heart, and kindles
a surpassing love of humanity;

it drives me out of doors, I get
this urge to stroll the streets;
soul yearns for soul, it peers around
for sweet, flowing gowns of white.

At such times I almost dissolve
from melancholy and yearning!
All cats are grey then; all women
Helens, all worth Troy's burning—

and as I came to the Drehbahn I saw,
in the shimmering of the moon,
an absolute babe, a gorgeous
full-breasted piece of womanhood.

Her face was round, sound as a bell,
her eyes were turquoise blue.
She had cheeks like roses, cherry lips,
her nose was quite reddish too.

On her head was perched a cap
of white linen, starched and bent
into a mural crown, complete
with towers and battlements.

She wore a white tunic that dangled
down, sheer, to her calves—
what calves!—while her ankles
resembled two Doric pillars.

A perfectly worldly naturalness
was revealed by her features;
but a rump that was superhuman
was proof of a higher creature.

She stepped right up and addressed me:
"Welcome back to the Elbe;
you've been absent thirteen years
but you're still your same old self.

You seek, maybe, the beautiful
souls you used to tryst with
so often, tittle-tattling all night
in this salubrious district.

Life devoured them—that monster,
that hundred-headed Hydra.
You'll find nothing of the old times,
or of your companions either.

You won't find those demure blossoms
your young heart set on a pedestal;
they flowered here—but wilted now,
the storm-blast stripped their petals.

Wilted, stripped, even trampled
beneath fate's brutal feet—
that's the way of the world, my friend,
with all that is lovely and sweet!"

"Who are you?"—I cried—"you gaze at me
like a dream from yesteryear.
Where do you live, great image of woman?
And may I accompany you there?"

The woman laughed, then interposed:
"You're mistaken—I'm a refined
upstanding, moral individual;
quite wrong; I'm not one of those.

I'm not one of those little mam'zelles,
or some kerb-crawler's Lorette.
Know this—I am *Hammonia*,
Hamburg's tutelary goddess!

You hesitate—perhaps you're shocked.
Once you were such a brave singer!
Do you still want to accompany me?
If so, let's wait no longer."

But at that I laughed aloud, and cried
"I'll follow you to your place—
lead on; I'd follow you
if you were holed up Hades!"

CAPUT 24

How I ascended the narrow front stairs
is beyond my power to say;
perhaps invisible spirits
floated me up the *escalier.*

There, in Hammonia's room,
the hours swiftly passed;
it seems the goddess had had a crush
on me for quite some time.

"You see," she said, "not too long since
the singer dearest to me
was the one who sang *Messias*
as he strummed his pious lyre.

And the bust of my Klopstock
still stands on the commode,
but for some years now it's served
merely as a bonnet-block.

You're my darling these days—a picture
hangs over my headboard.
Look, laurel leaves adorn
the frame of your splendid portrait.

Yet you've so often belaboured
my sons, I have to admit
that at times you've wounded me
deeply. That I can't permit

any longer—which is why I hope
the years have softened your violence
and endowed you with the gift
of suffering fools in silence.

But now, tell me how on earth
you came to travel to the north
at this time of year? It's winter,
and the weather's growing bitter."

"Oh my goddess!"—I answered—
"the thoughts of the heart that sleep
deepest in the ground are often
those which wake when expected least.

Outwardly life seemed good enough,
but at heart I was apprehensive.
That apprehension grew, daily—
I succumbed to homesickness.

The French air, which seems so light,
weighed down on me like lead;
I had to breathe in Germany,
or be suffocated to death.

I longed for the scent of peat-smoke
and German tobacco fumes;
my feet would itch, impatient
to tramp on German ground.

I sighed at night-time, longing
once more to see the old lady
who lives in Dammtor, and
little Lotte, her neighbour.

Also to see that noble old man
who used to upbraid me,
but was a generous guardian—for him,
too, many sighs escaped me.

I wanted to hear again, from his mouth,
the words "Foolish youth!"—
they had always seemed like a music
reverberating in my heart.

I yearned for the pale blue woodsmoke
that curls from German chimney-pots,
for Lower Saxony's nightingales,
its beechen green and melodious plots.

I even pined for those calvaries—
those stations of the cross; for
the cross of youth I used to drag,
and the crown of thorns I wore.

I wanted to weep where, long ago,
I shed tears of tribulation;
'Love of one's homeland', I believe,
is the name for this infatuation.

Fundamentally it's a sickness
which I don't like to mention,
an embarrassment; I shield
the wound from public attention.

I'm mortified by the rag-tag mob
who stir up hearts with cunning
by hauling their patriotism into view
with all its ulcers running.

Shameless, shabby beggars they are,
bullying you for charity;
for Menzel and his Swabians,
a penn'orth of popularity!

O goddess, today you find me
in such a melting mood;
I'm rather poorly—but if you tend
to me I'll soon improve.

Yes, I am ill—and you could
make the spirit much more willing
by fixing up a good cup of tea;
add rum to improve the blend."

CAPUT 25

The goddess mashed me some tea,
deftly skinking rum in it;
for herself, she just poured
out a glassful and drank it neat.

Then she leant her head against
my shoulder (so, incidentally,
crumpling her mural crown
somewhat) and spoke to me gently:

"I was often horrified—used to blench
at the thought of you in Paris—
Sin City, Gomorrah—unsupervised
among those frivolous French;

a *flaneur*, promenading without
a chaperone at your side—
some German publisher, say—
to act as a mentor and guide.

It has too many temptations,
that place; it's riddled with sylphides
who're unsound, so easy that a man
can be driven out of his wits.

Please don't go back there, stay with us.
Breeding and morals still count
here—we've a not inconsiderable
fund of quiet amusement—

stay with us in Germany. You'll find
us much improved since you left.
We've made great strides. You've noticed
some changes here yourself;

the censor isn't as powerful now,
Hoffmann's been tempered by the years
and his youthful zeal for chopping
your *Travel Sketches* has disappeared.

You're older and more temperate, too—
you've learned to let things go;
as a result, even your view of the past
will acquire a rosier glow,

because, well, to claim it was awful
was always to exaggerate.
A slave—as in Rome—could always
escape by immolation,

and freedom of thought was always
enjoyed by the broad masses;
restrictions only ever applied
to those who tried to use presses.

Rule by arbitrary decree
it wasn't; even the worst demagogue
was never stripped of citizenship
without due legal process.

So Germany was never that bad,
despite troubled times. I don't believe
a single soul ever truly *starved*
to death in a German prison.

At that time, too, there blossomed
so many fair and outward shows
of faith and genial warmth;
now all is negativity and doubt.

Practical, external freedom will soon
shrivelled up the Ideal, which we
upheld in our bosoms—it was
as pure as a lily's dream—

Our beautiful poetry withers,
it already has a touch of rigor
mortis; Freiligrath's Moorish king dies
when real ones find grave-diggers.

Our grandchildren will feed better,
but not in tranquil stillness;
a melodrama is on the way—
the idyll has a fatal illness.

Oh, if I thought you could keep mum
I'd unseal the Book of Fates
and let you see the times to come
in my enchanted looking-glass;

things I've never shown mortal men
would be flung open to you—
that is, your fatherland's future.
But—well, you can't hold your tongue."

"My God, O Goddess", I cried out,
"that would be the supreme delight!
Let me glimpse the Germany
to come. I'm a man—I'm discreet.

I'll swear you any vow you want;
bind me solemnly. I can bear it
if your knowledge must stay secret.
Just tell me; how should I swear it?"

"I want it sworn," she replied,
in the manner of Father Abraham
with his servant, Eliezer,
before he set off on his travels.

Lift my robe and set your hand
here beneath my thigh, and swear
to me your silence henceforth—
in speech and in writing."

An auspicious moment, that!
An atavistic wind of passion
shivered me as I swore the oath
after my forefather's fashion.

I lifted the robe of the Goddess up,
and set my hand beneath her thigh,
and solemnly promised silence henceforth—
in writing and in speech.

CAPUT 26

The Goddess's cheeks glowed all red.
(I think her alcoholic
intake had gone to her crown). Her
voice came slurred, thick, melancholic;

"I'm getting old. I was born on
the day Hamburg was founded.
Mother was the Herring Queen
where Elbe runs into the sea,

father was a great monarch—
Carolus Magnus his nomenclature—
cleverer than Frederick the Great
he was, and greater in stature.

His throne's in Aachen now—
the one for his investiture
that is—but the throne he ascended
at night came down to my mother.

She passed it on to me. I daresay
there's furniture that's finer,
but I wouldn't swap it for Rothschild's gold
or all the tea in China.

That old armchair there, in the corner—
see it? The one with ripped
leather covers, and the cushion-
stuffing all moth-corrupted?

Go over. Lift up the cushion.
Go on—lift it! Underneath
there's a circular opening.
Inside it you'll see a gazunder.

That's the enchanted cauldron;
that's where the magic powers brew.
If you stick you head over it
you'll catch a glimpse of the future.

Germany-to-be bubbles up
like a wavering phantasma,
but you mustn't shudder if the stuff
gives off a miasma—"

and she laughed, unnervingly.
Refusing to be deterred
I inquisitively stuck my head
over the dread hole, as she said.

As I've mentioned, owing to my oath
what I saw has been edited;
but dear God ! If I said what I *smelt*
my tale would scarcely be credited.

Even now I have a terror
of that presaging stink, which seemed
to be an unspeakable mix
of rancid cabbage and Russian leather.

Weeping Jesus! It seemed as if
they'd managed to mingle the stinks
of all the foulest flushings
from thirty-six septic tanks.

I know what Saint-Just told Weiland
at that meeting of the Committee:
"One cannot cure a great sickness
with attar of rose and musk"—witty,

but the reek of Germany to come
by my nasal precognition
would have overborne *anything*.)
I was poleaxed by its hum,

my senses swam... and when my eyes
opened, I was sitting back next
to the goddess. She'd crushed my head
to her generously-stacked chest;

her eyes were flashing, her lips were red,
her nostrils flaring wide—
I was gripped in a Bacchic half-nelson.
She sang, ecstatically fired,

"Stay with me in Hamburg; I *love* you!
We'll devour the oysters
and Rhenish of the here-and-now—
forget the shadowy future!

Don't let that stink intrude on
our joy! Dear, drop the seat—
I love you as no mortal woman
ever loved a German poet!

I'll kiss you... ah—I'm *trembling!*—
your genius enthrals me ;
it stupefies, it batters, it forces
my spirit to bend the knee

to it—and now it seems the street
is full of nightwatchmen; they chorus
serenades, epithalamiums—
Oh, you sweet provoker of lust!

Equerries are cantering up—
each one grips a flaring link;
they dressage in a fire-dance,
they curvett and prance and jink.

The worshipful, prudent senators
are arriving, aldermen in tow.
The *Bürgermeister* wants to speak;
he harrumphs and swallows.

Resplendent in their uniforms
come the *corps diplomatique*
to offer us discreet plaudits
on behalf of neighbouring states.

There's a deputation of lords spiritual
including rabbis and pastors—
but wait! Here comes Hoffmann as well
with his censor's scissors! Disaster!

The scissors are clacking in his hand,
he's flung himself crazily at
your body—he's sheared the flesh, and—
O! That was your choicest cut!"

CAPUT 27

So: whatever else transpired on that
never-to-be-forgotten night
I'll save for a fuller account
on some warm summer's day,

but this I will say: the older kind
of hypocrite, thank God, is dying;
it's sinking slowly into the grave
through the sheer weight of its lying.

A new generation is growing up
free of dissimulation and 'sin';
free in thought, free in desire—
I'll save my vision for them.

The new-fledged youth now understand
a poet's pride and worth.
They thaw themselves out at his heart
and bask in his radiant warmth.

My heart is loving like the light,
incorruptible and pure as fire;
the noblest Graces harmonised
the catgut of my lyre—

the very same lyre that was first
tuned up and strummed on by
my father, blest Aristophanes,
the Muses' blue-eyed boy;

it's the selfsame lyre with which
he once sang of Paisteteros
when he courted Basileia
and they both soared in the skies.

In the last caput I tried to sketch
the plot of *The Birds*—which is
generally agreed to be the best
of all my father's dramas.

The Frogs is good as well. There's
a German translation, being
played right now in Berlin
at the express wish of the king.

The king likes the play. This shows,
I think, excellent classical taste;
but the old king laughed a lot more
at contemporary croakers.

The king likes the play. Even so,
its author's health would worsen
if he were still alive, and found
himself in Prussia in person.

For Aristophanes wouldn't enjoy
our world that much; nor would
he be terribly pleased
to see gendarmes forming his Chorus.

The rabble, rather than applauding,
would be stirred up against him—
the police would be under orders
to keep him under surveillance.

O, King! I'm feeling well disposed
so here's some advice for free—
exalt dead poets, by all means,
but leave the living ones alone.

Don't affront the living poets!
They wield fire and brimstone
more fearful than Jove's thunderbolts
(which are a poet's invention).

Affront the Gods, the old and new,
the whole Olympian pantheon,
even all-highest Jehovah—
just don't incense the poets.

It's true that Gods take harsh revenge
on misbehaving humanity,
and that hellfire's hard to roast in
with any degree of urbanity,

yet there are saints who can free
sinners from torment. Requests
for mercy can be granted
through masses and pious bequests,

and when time ends, Christ will descend
to shatter Hell's portals—
however harsh the Last Judgement,
He will acquit many mortals—

yet there are hells from which
there can be no appeal—
even the Saviour can't harrow them;
no prayers there will avail.

Have you heard of Dante's *Inferno*?
Its savage *terza rima?*
Those shackled in obloquy there
will never find a redeemer—

no God, no Christ, can ransom them
from that singeing conflagration;
take care, then, lest you be consigned
to a similar damnation.

Notes:

Caput 1

l. 33. *I'll sing you a newer, better song*: can be interpreted as referring to *Deutschland* or a genuine political poetry Heine had yet to write, as opposed to the *Tendenzpoesie* of his contemporaries.

l. 38. *we won't put up with hunger.* What Heine called 'der grossen Suppenfrage' was the basis of his politics in *Deutschland.*

ll 42-4. *enough roses too... garden peas:* cf. *On the History of Religion and Philosophy in Germany* (1835), where Heine addresses the Babeuvists from a Saint Simonian point of view: 'We do not want to be sansculottes, nor simple citizens, nor venal presidents; we want to found a democracy of gods, equal in majesty, sanctity, and in bliss. You demand simple dress, austere morals, and unspiced pleasures, but we demand nectar and ambrosia, crimson robes, costly perfumes, luxury and splendour, the dancing of laughing nymphs, music and comedies.'

l. 57. *first kiss:* the hopes raised by the July Revolution of 1830.

l. 76. *the giant:* Antaeus, who in Greek mythology drew strength from his mother, the earth, each time he was thrown to the ground. Hercules finally defeated Antaeus by hanging him on the branches of a tree—an implicit crucifixion of poet and people.

Caput 2

l. 19. *a new God:* Barker Fairley refers to the immanent 'God of the Pantheists' mentioned by Heine in his poem 'Aug diesem Felsen bauen wir' / 'On this rock shall we build' and to his discussion of God in Book 2 of *On the History of German Religion and Philosophy.* When he was dying Heine returned to the idea of a personal God.

l. 28. *von Fallersleben:* August Heinrich Hoffmann von Fallersleben (1798-1874), poet and author of 'Deutschland, Deutschland über alles.' Von Fallersleben shared his publisher, Campe, with Heine, and was indirectly responsible for all of Campe's publications being banned by the Prussian government when his *Unpolitische Lieder* appeared in 1841. For all this, Heine is playing up the actual subversiveness of Von Fallersleben's work here for ironic effect.

l. 32. *Zollverein:* the pan-Germanic customs union established by Prussia in 1834. It gradually attracted many non-Prussian states and was instrumental in preparing the way for the Prussian-led unification of Germany in 1870.

Caput 3

l. 4. *Karl Mayer* (1786-1870): one of the many minor poets Heine takes a swipe at in *Deutschland*. His name is the German form of Carolus Magnus (Charlemagne).

l. 7. *Stukkert:* Swabian dialect form for Stuttgart.

l. 19. *Körner:* Theodor Körner (1791-1813), author of *Leier und Schwert* (1814).

l. 31-2. *the cosy Du still reminds them / of* Er*lier forelock-touching tones:* what Heine refers to as 'das alte Er' was a by-then-disused form of address to inferiors common in the eighteenth century; he is claiming that Prussians have had problems adapting to the more personal 'du' because of their rigidly militaristic and subordinated society.

l. 35. *pigtail:* the pigtail became a symbol of eighteenth century pedantry and militaristic rigidity (pigtails are associated with philistinism).

l. 37-9. *pickelhaube:* the pickelhaube, or spike-topped helmet, was introduced as part of a Gothicizing programme by the Prussian king Friedrich Wilhelm IV (1840-61).

l. 43. *Johanna von Montfaucon:* a play by von Kotzebue (1761-1819) set in the Middle Ages.

l. 44. *Romantic/Fouqué, Uhland, Tieck:* the best-known 'comic' rhyme in the poem, but not Heine's invention, since it comes from a poem by J. B. Rousseau. Friedrich de la Motte-Fouqué (1777-1843), Ludwig Uhland (1787-1862) and Ludwig Tieck (1773-1853) were older contemporaries of Heine and are discussed in his *The Romantic School*.

l. 62. *detestable bird:* the Prussian eagle.

l. 76. *'Long live the King!':* a double meaning - the winner of a marksmanship contest is called the *schützenkönig,* or shooting king.

Caput 4

l. 23. *the dark men:* Medieval Cologne's theologians were satirized in the humanist 'Dunkelmännerbriefe', the *Epistolae Obscurorum Virorum* (1515-17), to which Ulrich von Hutten contributed.

l. 27. *Hochstraaten…* Menzel: Jakob von Hochstraaten was the most prominent of the Cologne theologians. Wolfgang Menzel (1798-1873) was the editor of the *Literaturblatt* in Stuttgart from 1826 to 1849 ; he led the attack on Heine and others which led to the ban on the 'Young Germany' movement in 1835.

l. 36. *sectarian hatred:* in the original version the line read 'An ihrem Judenhasse' ('by its hatred of the Jews'). Heine changed 'Judenhasse' to 'Glaubenhasse' ('sectarian hatred') after he showed the lines to Wille, a liberal journalist, who observed, 'What business do you still have with Jews? Your sympathies are neither with their nationality nor their religion. And why must you, in the very work in which you ridicule one kind of nationalism, exhibit weakness for another?'

l. 49. *it's unfinished:* Cologne Cathedral had been incomplete since Luther's time, but the Romantic revival of interest in the Middle Ages and a reappraisal of Gothic style led to attempts to complete it. The two leading spirits behind the project were Joseph Görres (1776-1848) and Sulpice Boissereé (1783-1854). A Cathedral Association was founded and the remaining building work was completed between 1842 and 1880. As several commentators have pointed out, Heine himself contributed to their funds only two years before writing *Deutschland.*

l. 52. *protestant:* according to Barker Fairley the word is used 'in its least doctrinal sense'; the lower case conveys Heine's intentions here.

l. 61-8. *Liszt... a gifted monarch... Swabian jackasses:* On the day building activities restarted, in September 1842, Liszt gave a fundraising concert, the Prussian King Friedrich Wilhelm IV made a speech and Swabian supporters sent a cargo of building stone from Stuttgart. Heine's reference to the King's talents is not ironic — Friedrich Wilhelm was regarded as an intelligent, even gifted monarch — but, as Heine points out elsewhere, his good intentions were frustrated by the reactionary nature of Prussian society, and his uncertainty was in some ways worse than outright autocracy.

l. 83. *the Three Wise Men from the East:* the line 'Die heilgen drei Könge aus Morgenland' is the opening line of an early Heine poem. Legend had it that the bones of the 'Three Wise Men' were taken to Cologne from Italy in the twelfth century.

l. 86. *three iron cages:* in 1536 Johann von Leyden (the 'Tailor King') and two other Anabaptists were executed and their bodies displayed in cages hung from the tower of Saint Lamberti's church in Münster.

l. 97. *the Holy Eastern Alliance:* not just the magi of the Bible story, but the anti-democratic bloc or 'Holy Alliance' of Russia, Prussia and Austria-Hungary founded at the Congress of Vienna in 1815.

l. 104. *promised constitutional redress:* Friedrich Wilhelm III (1797-1840) promised his subjects a constitution, but refused to implement it.

Caput 5

l. 15. *I missed you thirteen years back:* according to Heine's
Confessions (1854) he did not see the river on the earlier occasion:
'On May 1st 1831 I crossed over the Rhine. I did not see the old river-
god of the Rhine and I contented myself with throwing my visiting-
card into the water. He sat, I am told, at the bottom of the stream
where he was studying again Meidner's *French Grammar*, for he had
under Prussian rule fallen back much in his French, and would work it
up again to provide against contingencies. I imagined that I heard him
conjugating below, *J'aime, tu aimes, il aime, nous aimons.* Whom
does he love, however? Not Prussians, in any event.'

l. 17. *choked on stone:* a reference to the 1841 dispute between
Hessen-Nassau and Hessen-Darmstadt, rival trading ports on the
Rhine, in which the former built a harbour at Biberich. In retaliation,
the latter sank 103 boats loaded with stone and blocked the harbour
entrance. The pretext for the shipment was that it had been intended
for Cologne Cathedral. Heine links the petty particularity of the
current German states and a reactionary medievalism.

l. 20. *Becker:* Nikolaus Becker (1804-45), author in 1840 of an
anti-French patriotic song beginning 'They shall not have it, our
free German Rhine.' The French politician Thiers, among others,
had suggested that the Rhine should be the Franco-German border.
Sentiment against France was strong in Germany at the time.

l. 49. *de Musset:* Alfred de Musset (1810-57), who replied with;
'Nous avons eu votre Rhin allemand' ('We have had your "German
Rhine."')

l. 61. *and swapped white ones for red:* According to Barker Fairley,
La Grande Encyclopédie gives the date 1829 for the introduction of
the 'pantalon garance'; the change was made in order to support the
French madder industry.

l. 66. *Fischte:* Fichte is misspelt by Heine to approximate French
pronunciation.

l. 72. *Hengstenbergists:* Ernst Wilhelm Hengstenberg (1802-68) was
an anti-semitic Christian theologian; in his *Evangelische Zeitung*
he attacked Goethe for religious unorthodoxy and Heine for his
Jewishness.

Caput 6

l. 4. *Georg Harris* (1780-1838): one of Paganini's managers and a
minor author; he published *Paganinisana* in 1830.

l. 61-72. *You're judge and jury... I'm... the deed / to which your thought has bound you:* Heine was a great believer not merely in the primacy of thought, but also in the inevitability of the physical embodiment of thought. A story in his *Religion and Philosophy in Germany* tells of a Frankenstein-type mechanic who creates a creature which pursues him, demanding a soul. But how much worse, Heine adds, is the reverse situation: 'It is appalling when the bodies we have created ask us for a soul. Yet it is far more horrible, appalling and uncanny when we have created a soul which then demands its body and pursues us with this demand ... the idea wants to become a deed, the word to become flesh.'

Caput 7

l. 15. *O German soul:* cf. Schiller's 'Der Antritt des neuen Jahrhunderts': 'Freiheit ist nur in dem Reich der Träume' ('Freedom is only found in the kingdom of dreams').
ll. 21-4. *France and Russia ... our indisputable territories:* from Jean-Paul (Richter) (1763-1825) 'Providence has given to the French the Empire of the land, to the English that of the sea, and to the Germans that of the air.'
l. 43. *as we passed a doorpost:* cf. Exodus 12:7, with Moses's injunction to the Israelites to anoint the doorposts of their houses with the blood of a lamb so that the inhabitants will not be harmed by the Angel of Death. Whereas the blood-markings in Exodus are protective, in Heine they are the reverse.
l. 103. *If you don't leave you'll be forced out:* see Goethe's 'Erlkönig'; 'Und bist du nicht willig, so brauch ich Gewalt' ('And if you are unwilling, I must use force'). Again, Heine reverses the situation; it is the man who threatens the ghost, although a non-human figure actually executes his wishes.

Caput 8

l. 16. *Atalanta's golden apples:* according to Greek myth, Atalanta defeated all her suitors by challenging to a foot-race. Hippomenes finally won her hand by throwing down three golden apples during their race, which she lost when she stopped to pick them up.
l. 20. *in May of '31:* Heine is referring to the Revolution of 1830-31 which affected territory around France and brought Louis Philippe, the 'Citizen King' to power there. This was the event which decided him on his permanent move to live in Paris.

l. 25. *Their skinflint lordships:* an ms. variant of this line reads: 'Sie dachten: Die Preussen, das magere Volk' ('They thought: Prussians, that skinny race').

l. 46. *the English worms preferred... a* graver *man*: as elsewhere, Heine has a low opinion of England but a high regard for Shakespeare (*Atta Troll* and *Deutschland* both have Shakespearian surtitles); the allusion is to *Romeo and Juliet* and the dying Mercutio's 'Ask for me tomorrow, you shall find me a grave man.' See also *Ideas: The Book of Le Grand:* 'Britannia! You own the sea. But the sea has not water enough to wash away the disgrace that this great man bequeathed to you with his death ... you yourself were the Sicilian assassin hired by a conspiracy of kings to take secret revenge on the man of the people for what the people had once done publicly to one of your own kind —and he was your guest, sitting by your fireside— '

Caput 9

l. 6. *every traditional German dish:* here, as elsewhere in the poem, Heine uses food to give force to a series of observations and broader judgements on German society and culture. Drawing on Rabelaisian example, Heine treats those appetites and functions of the flesh which are dismissed as 'low' and gross in official discourse (food, drink, sex, defecation) as potentially subversive.

Caput 10

l. 13. *the Westphalian Club:* the 'Westfalia' was a student drinking society, joined by Heine at Göttingen University in 1824.

l. 24. *Quarter-blow... tierce:* fencing strokes.

Caput 11

l. 1. *Teutoburg Forest:* wooded country between the Ems and the Lippe where, according to Tacitus, Varus and his Roman legions were defeated by Hermann (Arminius), leader of the Cheruscan tribe, in 9 AD, thus securing the independence of the Germanic tribes from Rome.

l. 11. *Teutonic liberty... Roman chattels:* when Heine was studying Roman Law he joked in a letter that if the Romans had won the battle of the Teutoberg Forest his task would have been easier, an idea developed in *Ideas: The Book of Le Grand;* 'The Romans would never have had time to conquer the world if they had first had to learn

Latin.'

l.15. *quirites:* Roman citizens.

ll. 17-20 *Neander:* August Neander (1789-1850) was a disciple of Schleiermacher and professor of Theology at Berlin. Heine makes Hengstenberg a *haruspex* and Neander an *augur* because these are Roman soothsayers who made their prophesies by reading patterns made by the guts of disemboweled animals and by the flight of birds; they thus represent worldly and speculative theology respectively.

l. 22. *Birch-Pfeiffer:* Charlotte Birch-Pfeiffer (1800-68), actress and writer of sentimental dramas.

l. 25. *Raumer:* Friedrich von Raumer (1784-1873), Berlin professor of political science, whose chief work was a history of the Hohenstaufens. In his *Conditions in France* Heine admitted that 'he is still the best of all the middle-ranking authors.'

l. 28. *Flaccus Horatius:* Horace, the Latin poet.

l. 29. *Father Jahn:* Friedrich Ludwig ('Turnvater') Jahn (1778-1852), founder of a patriotic student movement with an emphasis on gymnastics ; their motto was 'Frisch, fromm, fröhlich, frei' ('Fresh, devout, happy, free').

l. 31. *Me hercule:* 'by Hercules'. Massmann: Hans Christian Massmann (1797-1874) was a Berlin professor, politically associated with Jahn.

l. 41. *Schelling:* F. W. J. von Schelling (1775-1854), Idealist aesthetician and philosopher. *Seneca*: (d. 65 AD), Roman philosopher and poet who committed suicide by opening his veins to escape a worse death at the hands of Nero.

l. 43. *Cornelius:* Peter von Cornelius (1783-1867), religious genre painter.

l. 44. *cacatum non est pictum:* 'You don't make pictures by shitting.'

l. 64. *Detmold:* on the edge of the Teutoberg Forest.

Caput 12

l. 20. *gesticulated, struck the pose*: this caput is a reminder of Heine's unorthodoxy. The rhetoric and stale jargon echo apprehensions about the place of culture in a society of primitive, subsistence communism which he expresses elsewhere.

l. 41. *The sheep's clothing:* Matthew 7:15; 'Beware of false prophets, which come to you in sheep's clothing, but inwardly they are ravening wolves.'

l. 50. *howl along with the wolves:* this line has been read as dangerously irresponsible. Apart from the ironic context, however,

this use of the wolves and lambs is part of a literary tradition which stretches from the Bible to the present day; see for example, Hans Magnus Enzensberger's 'the wolves defended against the lambs', an attack on postwar West German materialism and complacency.
l. 56. *Kolb:* Gustav Kolb (1798-1865), editor of the *Augsberger Allgemeine Zeitung,* which published articles by Heine (sometimes cut).

Caput 13

l. 1. *The sun rose over Paderborn... exasperation*: Meno Spann speaks of the 'painful jauntiness' of the opening of this Caput, adding that Heine goes on to 'take Christ to task as a fellow publicist who miscalculated.'
ll. 9-10. *Sisyphus... Danaides:* in Greek mythology, Sisyphus was condemned to roll a large stone uphill which promptly rolled back down again after reaching the summit; the Danaides were condemned to eternally pour water into a leaking tub.
l. 16. *that man who was crucified:* as a Jew whose baptism caused him much soul-searching, Heine's attitude to Christ was a complicated one. When Jesus appears in Heine's pages, he does so as a Jew, reared in the religion of Israel, drawing on the Israelite heritage for help in performing his world-historical task. He also appears as a *bon dieu citoyen*, a true democrat whom the narrator (in *The Town of Lucca*) professes to love beyond any other god. That is, the historical Christ is turned against institutionalized Christianity, in line with the general tendency of the poem to avoid a Jewish persona.

Caput 14

l. 4. *'Sun, you accusing flame!'*: the theme of the sun as an accuser is familiar in German folk literature; Fairley notes its appearance in Chamisso's ballad 'Die Sonne bringt es ein Tag.'
l. 15. *lynch mob;* closest equivalent of Heine's 'Vehme'. These were secret courts which existed in the Middle Ages for the preservation of peace, suppression of crime and maintenance of Catholicism; they were particularly active in Westphalia.
l. 33. *She had to tend the geese:* 'The Little Goose Girl' is a story from the Grimm Brothers' *Kinde-und Hausmärchen* (1812-14).
l. 51. *Redbeard:* the Holy Roman Emperor Friedrich I (1152-90).
l. 57. *Kyffhäuser:* a mountain in Thüringen. Its association with the Redbeard legend had been recently revived by a poem by Rückert,

'Die alte Barbarossa.'
Caput 15

ll. 6-7. *'Three Riders Gallop Through The Gate'* / 'Es reiten drei Reiter zum Tor hinau': the opening line of the poem 'Drei Reiter am Tor' in *Des Knaben Wunderhorn*.

l. 79. *chi va piano va sano:* equivalent to the German 'Eile mit Weile' and the English 'More haste, less speed.' Literally, he who acts cautiously acts safely.

Caput 16

l. 12. *the Seven Years' War:* 1756-1763.

l. 13. *He asked after Moses Mendelssohn:* Heine plays on the disparity between Barbarossa the icon of militant nationalism (and hence of contemporary nationalist anti-semites), and the fact that the historical Barbarossa was favourably inclined towards Jews within his territories. In calling Moses Mendelssohn's wife Rebecca, Heine knew he was bending historical fact himself (her name was Fromet). The change helps complete a sequence of Old Testament names for the Mendelssohn family (Moses, Rebecca, Abraham, Leah), a sequence which is then significantly broken by Felix, Moses' grandson, the composer. As Prawer puts it, 'The change shows how the family had grown away from its Judaism to assume the classical Christian heritage of Europe.'

l. 14. *Karschin:* Anna Luisa Karsch (1722-91) wrote poetry. Her daughter, Karoline Luise von Klenke (1754-1812), and her granddaughter, Helmine Christine von Chézy, also wrote. Heine knew Helmine well.

l. 30. *Countess du Barry:* Marie Jeanne Bécu (1746-1793), Mistress of Louis XV.

l. 35. *The Sixteenth:* Louis XVI (1747-1793).

l. 51. *Monsieur Guillotin:* Joseph-Ignace Guillotin (1738-1814), a doctor who perfected the guillotine.

l. 69. *Who are you, for that matter ..?*: as in Caput 17, Heine makes much of the contradictory nature of Redbeard as a symbol of coming revolution. Redbeard's outburst has been triggered off by the speaker's glib enumeration of executions and his use of the familiar 'du'.

l. 91. *Burstenschaft:* the organization of German students which grew out of the anti-French Wars of Liberation and aimed at moral reform and national unity. It took as its colours the 'black-red-gold' Heine mentions here and elsewhere.

Caput 17

l. 29. *Charles the Fifth's Star Chamber / and his penal regulations:*
the Halsgericht, a criminal court established by Charles V in 1582.
l. 33. *Holy Roman Empire:* ostensibly lasted from 962 to 1806, but
had disintegrated as a political unit long before its demise.
l. 41. *chivalry-in-spats:* Heine's coinage is 'Kamaschenrittertum'; it
sums up the traveller's preference for a genuine past, a Middle Ages
with all their inequality and oppression, to the parody of the past in
which Friedrich IV was then engaged. Prawer notes that this lament
for passing greatness, the concern with style, has affinities with
Nietzsche rather than with republicanism. The French text is more
explicit than the German: 'cette chevallerie en uniforme prussien.'
l. 45. *Close down the theatres:* as Fairley observes, Heine in this
Caput is recalling Barbarossa in terms that reject him.

Caput 18

l. 1. *A safe stronghold our Minden is still:* Heine adapts the opening
two lines of Luther's hymn, 'Ein feste Burg ist unser Gott,' which
has become in English 'A safe stronghold our God is still.' *Minden:*
in Westfalia, a province given to Prussia at the Congress of Vienna
(1815).
l. 14. *Odysseus:* see *The Odyssey*, Book 9, ll. 239-44: 'Next thing,
/ he heaved up and set into position the huge door stop, / a massive
thing; no twenty-two of the best four-wheeled / wagons could have
taken that weight off the ground and carried it, / such a piece of sky-
towering cliff that was he set over / his gateway.' Odysseus and his
companions escaped from Polyphemus (the Cyclops), by blinding
him while he was sleeping. Apart from the inference, as in Caput 2,
that Prussian subversion-hunting is oppressive but also blinkered, even
stupid, there is also the parallel between Heine, travelling incognito
('Herr No-one'), and Odysseus who tells Polyphemus that his name is
'Outis' ('No-one').
l. 40. *Faubourg-Poissonière:* Paris district ; Heine moved there in
1841.
l. 59. *gobbling the liver from my breast:* Zeus punished Prometheus,
who stole fire from heaven in order to help humanity, by chaining him
to a rock while a vulture devoured his liver.
ll. 67-8. *the open country / in the vicinity of Bückeburg:* Bückeburg
was in the 'Freistaat' Schaumberg-Lippe. The journey leaves Prussian
territory and the traveller's relief is made clear.

Caput 19

l. 1. *Danton:* Georges Danton (1759-1794), French revolutionary
and leader of the Girondins; when told to flee the country to escape
the clutches of Robespierre he is said to have replied 'Est-ce qu'on
emporte sa patrie à la semelle de son soulier?'

l. 23. *the King:* Ernst Augustus, Duke of Cumberland, who became
King of Hanover in 1837. Prawer notes that Heine's first description
of Ernst August of Hanover was toned down to ease the poem past the
censor; he was initially described as an 'English Tory, proud, hunting-
Junker, / A scrawny despiser of the people.' The resort to irony had no
effect, since the Hamburg censor deleted most of this Caput anyway.

ll. 35-6. *our good friends'/Liberal lack...:* German liberals who were
less than forceful in their opposition to feudalism. Many, as Heine's
lines suggest, would shy away from revolution in 1848.

Caput 21

l. 1. *burnt-down half:* this Caput refers to the fire of 1842 (which
destroyed Heine's mother's house).

l. 9. *the printshop:* the Langhoffsche.

l. 13. *Dreckwall:* a street in Hamburg.

l. 35. *Banko:* the Banko-Wert, or value in the currency of Hamburg.

l. 70. *this deadly bird:* the Prussian eagle again. Prussia was trying to
get Hamburg, which was, as the poem later points out, a free city or
'Republic' (like Venice), to join its Zollverein.

Caput 22

l. 13. *my old friend Gudel:* the first of several self-references — Gudel
is the beloved of Heine's character Hirsch-Hyazinth, the valet of
the ex-Jewish, self-styled Marchese di Gumpelino in *Die Bäder von
Lucca / The Baths of Lucca* (1830).

l. 18. *the paper merchant:* Eduard Michaelis, another Jewish Hamburg
acquaintance.

l. 21. *Halle:* Adolf Halle, a much-disliked brother-in-law whose name
is indicated by a dash in published editions of the poem; Prawer
speaks of Heine's 'rather heartless fun' at the expense of a man who
had recently suffered a mental breakdown.

l. 25. *my old censor:* Friedrich Ludwig Hoffmann, the Hamburg
censor from 1822-48.

l. 35. *Gumpelino*: the Jewish banker Lazarus Gumpel (d.1843), the original for the Marchese di Gumpelino.

l. 42. *that crooked Adonis:* the mock-heroic Jewish reference to Gumpelino is followed, as Prawer points out, by 'an equally mock-heroic classical Greek reference in a complementary sketch of a poor street-vendor, who is also... no longer to be seen.'

l. 45. *Sarras:* Campe's dog.

l. 47. *Campe:* Julius Campe (1792-1867), Heine's regular publisher (Hoffmann und Campe, Hamburg) from the *Reisebilder* on.

l. 54. *they also eat heartily:* in 'The Memoirs of Herr Schnabelewopski', published in four collections of incidental pieces titled *Der Salon* (1834-40), Heine noted: 'As individuals the Hamburgers differ concerning religion, politics, and science, but they are in complete accord when it comes to eating. No matter how much Hamburg's Christian theologians may quarrel about the significance of the Last Supper, they all agree on the value of today's dinner.'

l. 60. *temple:* The less orthodox Hamburg Jews had left the synagogue in 1816 and formed a Tempelverein (Temple Association).

l. 64. *aristoscratchy* (original *aristokrätzig*): a typical Heine portmanteau word; the synagogue Jews are accused of combining their aristocratic sentiments with abrasiveness, and with the kind of insanitary scratching habits that lead to psoriasis ('krätzig' means 'scratchy').

Caput 23

ll. 11-20. *Chaufpié... Wille... Fuchs:* a doctor, a journalist and a schoolteacher respectively. Wille had duelling scars on his face from his student days and read *Deutschland* before its publication.

l. 20. *Canova:* Antonio Canova (1757-1822) an Italian sculptor.

l. 21. *Amphitryo:* Amphitryon, a Greek mythological figure, who is a generous host in Molière's comedy of the same name.

l. 53. *Drehbahn:* street in Hamburg's red light district.

l. 55. *an absolute babe:* Hammonia, Hamburg's tutelary goddess and patron saint ('Hammonia' is Hamburg latinized). Laura Hofrichter claimed in her 1963 study of Heine: 'In the three years he spent in Hamburg (1815-1819) his distrust turned into hatred; "Many a German poet has sung himself into a consumption here." All he could do, he added, was to rhyme "wretched" with "miserable." His first impressions seem to have remained with him. Some years later he declined an invitation to Hamburg, saying: "I am glad to hear that you seem to be happy in Hammonia's arms. This fair lady isn't to my taste. Her gold-embroidered dress doesn't deceive me: I know

she has a dirty shift on her yellow body and that, amorously melting
and sighing 'Rindfleisch, Banko,' she falls on the breast of whoever
offers her the most." So deeply rooted was this image in his mind
that twenty years later — he was never forgiven for it — he depicted
Hammonia, Hamburg's patron saint, as a prostitute.'
l. 63. *a mural crown... battlements*: as on Hamburg's coat of arms.
ll. 77-8. *the beautiful / souls*: these words have had a special
connotation in German since Weimar, for example, Goethe's
'Bekenntnisse einer schönen Seele.'
ll. 88, 92. *the storm-blast stripped their petals... all that is lovely and
sweet*: Allusions to famous scenes at the end of Lessing's Emilia
Galotti and Thekla's epitaph on her lover in Schiller's Wallenstein,
which 'create a humour of incongruity'.
l. 102. *Lorette*: nickname for those prostitutes in Paris who frequented
the neighbourhood of Notre-Dame de Lorette.

Caput 24

l. 11. *Messias*: a religious epic by Friedrich Gottlieb Klopstock (1724-
1803).
ll. 50-3. *the old lady... little Lotte... that noble old man*; Heine refers
to his mother, his sister Charlotte Embden and his Uncle Salomon.
l. 61. *the pale blue woodsmoke*: a motif for homesickness used by
Heine elsewhere, originating in *The Odyssey*, Book 1, ll. 57-9; 'and
yet Odysseus, / straining to get sight of the very smoke uprising / from
his own country, longs to die.'
l. 83. *Menzel and his Swabians*: as with the earlier references to the
Swabian poets Meyer and Mezel, Heine mocks a group of poets
which also included Gustav Pfizer (who had attacked Heine in 1838)
and Justinus Kerner.

Caput 25

l. 18. *sylphides:* 'Sylphiden', in Greek mythology creatures of the air;
here prostitutes.
l. 47. *stripped of citizenship:* of the 'Staatskokarde' in the original;
this was a kind of ribbon or rosette worn in the hat as a badge. The
removal of the cockade was a penalty introduced by Friedrich IV,
depriving the offender of civic rights.
l. 63. *Freiligrath's Moorish King:* Ferdinand Freiligrath (1810-
1876), poet and patriot, and author of 'Der Mohrenfürst'. The poem
tells of an African king who is captured in battle and who reappears

in captivity as a drummer in a French circus. In 1846 Heine half-apologized to Freiligrath for satirizing him here (and in *Atta Troll*).
l. 67. *melodrama:* 'Spektakelstück', a noisy play, often with a medieval plot.
l. 86. *in the manner of Father Abraham:* cf. Genesis, 24:2; 'And Abraham said unto his eldest servant of his house, that ruled over all that he had, Put, I pray thee, thy hand under my thigh. And I will make thee swear...' Heine's reference is a characteristic mixture of his intimate understanding of the workings of faith and ironic subversion.

Caput 26

l. 10. *Carolus Magnus:* according to tradition Charlemagne established an outpost at the mouth of the Elbe which became Hamburg.
l. 19. *Rothschild:* the banking house of the Rothschild family, founded in the eighteenth century, at the height of its power in Heine's time.
l. 52. *thirty-six septic tanks:* a reference to the thirty-six German states.
l. 53. *Saint-Just:* Heine attributes this saying to the French revolutionary Antoine de Saint-Just (1767-94), speaking as a member of the Comité de Salut Public: 'Ce n'est pas avec du musc et de l'eau que l'on peut guérir la grande maladie sociale.' There are variants of the aphorism, however, which has also been attributed to Mirabeau and Chamfort.

Caput 27

l. 23. *Aristophanes:* Aristophanes (fl. 450 B.C.) was the greatest of Greek comic dramatists and a particular favourite of Heine.
l. 85. *singeing conflagration:* takes us back to 'Sun, you accusing flame' in Caput 14, and the figure of Caput 6 who enacts the poet's thoughts.

Futher Reading:

Hal Draper, *Complete Poems of Heinrich Heine: a modern English version* (Suhrkamp, 1982).

Barker Fairly, *Heinrich Heine: an interpretation* (Clarendon Press, 1954).

Jost Hermand and Robert C. Holub, eds., *Heinrich Heine's contested identities: politics, religion and nationalism in nineteenth century Germany* (Peter Land, 1999).

S.S.Prawer, *Heine's Jewish Comedy* (Clarendon Press, 1983).

T.J.Reed, *Deutschland: A Winter's Tale*, with translation, introduction and notes (Angel Books, 1997).

Nigel Reeves, *Heinrich Heine: poetry and politics* (OUP, 1974).

Jeffery L.Sammons, *Heinrich Heine* (Metzler, 1991).

Anna Spencer, *Heinrich Heine* (Twayne, 1982).